Gold Minds

The Psychology of Winning in Sport

GOLD MINDS

Brian Miller

The Crowood Press

First published in 1997 by
The Crowood Press Ltd
Ramsbury, Marlborough
Wiltshire SN8 2HR

British Library Cataloguing in Publication Data

A catalogue record for this book is available from the British Library.

ISBN 1 86126 100 4

Photo previous page: multiple Olympic champion Steve Redgrave shares a
moment of victory with coach Jurgen Grobler.

Note: throughout this book 'he', 'him' and 'his' are used as neutral pronouns
and refer equally to males and females.

Typeset by MultiMedia Works Ltd, Gloucester
Printed and bound in Great Britain by WBC Book Manufacturers,
Mid Glamorgan

Contents

Foreword

Brian Miller has been the guiding force behind the British Olympic Association's (BOA) psychology support programme since the Psychology Steering and Advisory Groups were formed in 1990. His reputation as a world-leading sports psychologist was certainly known to me before we met. I quickly realized that this was the man to head up an area of sports science which was perhaps lacking the BOA support it needed.

My experience as a coach had shown psychology to be arguably the pivotal support science for all athletic performance at world level. Unless the mental preparation of an athlete has been tuned to the level required, gold medals at any Olympic Games (or World Championships) will remain a dream. It has to be accepted that no matter what their level of skill, or the extent of their physical preparation, an athlete who has neglected mental training will not deliver to their full potential.

Brian Miller was appointed the BOA's first Consultant Sports Psychologist. He has since brought to the BOA an awareness of the value of the science to athletes, coaches, team managers and even administrators at the Olympic Games. We have all been influenced by his pragmatic approach and the gift he has for applying seemingly complex concepts and techniques into the real world of the athlete. Brian has worked with some seventy Olympic medalists from the Olympic sports and has influenced the preparation of World and Olympic champions from thirteen different sports. This vast experience is evidenced throughout *Gold Minds*.

The book makes fascinating reading. Every page gives personal stories from some of the world's greats, covering the whole range of sports. Insights are given into the thoughts of Olympic medalists and we are provided with an insight into their mental checklists of preparation, evidence of Miller's attention to detail. For my part, I shall revisit the sections on the legendary Miller's 'what ifs', the crucial importance of mental toughness, and the process involved in the post-Games analysis.

I would suggest that this book is essential reading for athletes who aspire to fulfil their innate potential, for coaches who want to learn from the archives of success, and for support staff who work with athletes wishing to understand more clearly what sports psychology can offer.

Kevin Hickey MBE
Technical Director, British Olympic Association

Introduction

You can go on court some days and feel so sharp and so alert that the ball comes over the net looking as big as a soccer ball, and you think to yourself that there's no way I can make a mistake. Other days you go out and play as if you're in a fog, unsure of everything. Can I explain the difference? I wish I could, but I can't.

Rod Laver, all-time tennis great

It is not possible to prescribe a system of mental preparation that works for *all* athletes, *all* teams or *all* sports. While the principles of mental preparation may be generic, the practical application, by necessity, has to be specific. It needs to be an all-encompassing, bespoke system. Any mental training system should be integrated with the physical and the technical training programme. It should be co-ordinated by the coach, and it should fit in with the overall objectives of the competitive schedule.

Unfortunately, too many texts on sport psychology simply outline various mental techniques and skills, and the coach and or the athlete is left to work out where, when and if these techniques should be applied.

Johnnie Searle (l), coach Steve Gunn, Greg Searle (r) and cox Garry Herbert after winning Olympic gold in 1992.

The AIMS System

The AIMS System was originally developed by the author, and subsequently modified in the 1980s. The acronym stands for Acquiring Individual Mental Skills and includes a focus on tailoring the programme to the needs of the individual athlete. The AIMS programme was developed on the basis of equal expertise, namely, that the coach, the athlete and the sport psychologist each has a contribution to make with regards to the psychological preparation of the athlete. The psychologist should never assume that he has a monopoly on good ideas in this area. Similarly the coach and the athlete have to appreciate that within the model of equal expertise, the psychologist has something important to offer. The trio works together to ensure that the athlete moves through a fairly predictable transition process. The steps or progressions within the AIMS programme are: Innocence, Awareness, Competence and Excellence. Everyone involved with an athletic career is obliged to help to move the athlete through these stages with as little grief as possible. The goal is to have the athlete performing in the category known as Excellence as often as possible.

The British Olympic Association regularly holds study days for the sport psychologists who are members of its Psychology Advisory Group. These days have allowed most of the UK's top sport psychologists to swap ideas on how they work with elite performers. These events have led to a great sharing of information, and one consistent theme revolves around the timing of any psychological input with athletes and coaches. That is, identifying where and when a psychologist should get involved with athletes and coaches.

It has previously been suggested that there are six time-based phases involved in any good mental training system (Miller, 1985), and this is a pattern that has been adopted by other applied sport psychologists in Britain. The identified phases are as follows:

Long-term preparation for sport: a period lasting from four to twelve years and focusing on the long journey from novice to international competitor. This period is typified by a long, slow and often monotonous climb to the elite level. The physical training sessions required to make it at this level are often strenuous, arduous and boring. Athletes are often faced with problems relating to the sustaining of motivation and of being able to work through the 'lows' in order to reach the 'highs' of their competitive careers.

Sadly, it also has to be acknowledged that injury in sport is relevant for most athletes when considering their long-term involvement in it. Most athletes will be injured at some stage in their career and there are well defined skills and techniques which need to be acquired by athletes when this happens.

Long-term preparation for a specific competition: a period lasting for the final twelve to twenty-four months before a major event. Perhaps the best examples relate to preparation for the Olympic Games. Certainly specific preparation for many of the British squads in Atlanta started in 1993 or 1994. Issues such as the high temperatures and humidity, the American culture, and the abundance of fast foods in the USA were being openly discussed at this stage. Chapter 7 includes detailed examples of how the British and Australian teams have prepared for the Olympic Games.

Short-term preparation for a specific competition: a period lasting from the final few weeks to the last few seconds before an event. Much of the attention during this phase is centred on allowing the competitor to reproduce his or her best performance in the highly pressurized environment that is called the Olympic Games. Much of the work deals with teaching athletes to be able to handle their nerves and not become distracted or side-tracked by other issues. It is about teaching athletes to focus on the appropriate cues and issues at a time when all else around them seems to be getting out of control.

Competition focus: a period lasting the entire duration of the match, race or trial. During this period of the actual competition it is vital that athletes focus on the correct stimuli and concentrate on the task at hand. This may be difficult when one is competing to win an Olympic gold in front of 100,000 spectators and millions of television viewers.

Post-competition focus: the period lasting for the hours or days after the competition. For athletes who are continuing in their sport after a specific competition it is important that, win, lose or draw, lessons are learned from any competitive situation. One aspect of this relates to how athletes attribute success or failure. Ideally, athletes should be taught to accept responsibility for both.

Retirement: the period that follows the announcement of a retirement, typically lasting at least twelve months. This is a topic that has only recently been seen as important by sporting bodies around the world. Some athletes retire from sport and are happy to do so. They see retirement as a form of rebirth and are happy to get on with the next phase of their life. Unhappily, some athletes are not well prepared for their exit and view retirement as a form of dying. The Americans call this the 'hero to zero syndrome'. There have been many instances where retiring athletes have struggled to adjust to 'normal' life as an 'average' citizen. Stories of substance abuse, behavioural problems and even attempted suicides are common.

The Mental Edge

When an athlete competes in a major event he or she competes against other people who are fit, strong, flexible, powerful and skilful. All of the competitors have devoted time and energy to becoming top-class performers. But in a particular event, of course, there is only ever one champion and another couple of athletes who each receive a medal. Often, the difference between a medal and tenth place is only a matter of centimetres or fractions of a second.

Interviews with the athletes who succeed at the highest level focus on which aspect of their preparation made them different from everyone else. Nine times out of ten, these athletes refer to some mental edge or some psychological toughness that gave them an advantage. If an athlete wants to compete against others from around the world, then he needs to think carefully about mental preparation for both competition and training. It is not enough to expect to win simply by covering more mileage than the next athlete, or because he has lifted heavier weights. In the final analysis, it is often more important that he kept his head in the stressed environment of top-class competition. My work with elite athletes from twenty-three sports and seven countries has been based around the policy of preparing them for exactly that. During the life to date of the AIMS programme I have worked with more than seventy Olympic medalists from such sports as track and field, rowing, hockey, judo, shooting and canoeing. More than 3,000 international athletes have been exposed to all or some of the AIMS programme, and they have included world or Olympic champions from thirteen sports.

The Success Cycle

I first started my work on the psychological preparation for competitors in the early 1980s. I was influenced by many teachers in the field of applied sport psychology and these key people came from the USA, Canada, Australia, the United Kingdom and, most importantly, the former East Germany. The successful East German approach to psychology in sport was based around something called the Success Cycle and I was, and still am, a great fan of it. During the 1970s and the 1980s the East German system was arguably the most effective in world sport.

The Success Cycle shows the relationship between how an athlete feels about him or herself and how he or she is likely to perform in future events.

When speaking to an athlete we could say,

> If you have a positive self-image, you are more likely to have a positive attitude and this in turn is likely to lead to higher expectations of yourself. This tends to lead to improved behaviour (like getting to bed a little earlier or eating correctly), and because of these improvements the level of performance increases. Consequently, your self-image is enhanced and everything moves along nicely. But the effects of a negative self-image can be just as powerful, so it's important that you learn to keep the cycle moving upwards rather than downwards. The easiest way to ensure that this

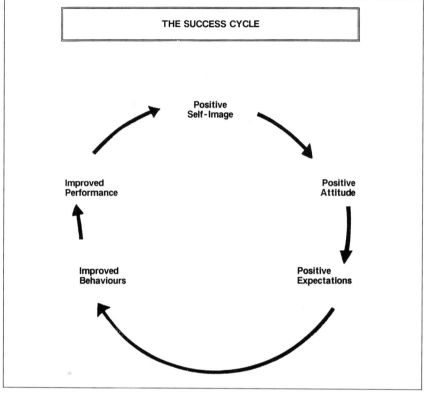

Fig 1

happens is to make sure that you're getting the most out of all training sessions and competitions.

During the last sixteen years I have made use of the Success Cycle in developing the programme known as AIMS. This book is designed to offer an insight into how successful performers from a range of sports have prepared for the major events. It will focus on how they have moved around the different elements of the Success Cycle and where and how the AIMS programme fits in.

The summary is that they are highly goal-oriented individuals and that the athletes have been focused on achieving their own personal version of the Success Cycle. The following chapters will deal with a number of discrete yet related topics, and it is hoped that the reader will enjoy the experience of sharing some of the secrets of *The Gold Minds*.

CHAPTER ONE

Goal-Setting

I feel that the most important step in any major accomplishment is setting a specific goal. This enables you to keep your mind focused on your goal and off the many obstacles that will arise while you're striving to do your best.
Kurt Thomas, Olympic gymnastics champion

If we do what we did yesterday we will be beaten, if we do what others are doing today we can be competitive, but if we fill every day with initiative, we will be the best.
Rob De Castella, world champion marathon runner

You reach the finish line one step at a time, one day at a time, and with the understanding that it will take many steps and many days to ensure you get there first. You achieve your goal one step at a time, focused and diligent, always moving forward.
Muhammad Ali, world and Olympic champion boxer

One way of helping to make sure that athletes continue to progress through the Success Cycle is to set goals and targets for them. Ideally, the athletes should have a significant input into establishing these goals for themselves. The adage used within the AIMS programme is 'if it's to be; it's up to me!' Athletes are taught that success comes in cans, not cannots, and that they have to strive for achievement. They have to *decide* to be outstanding and they have to be driven by the Japanese concept of *kaizen* – striving for continual improvement. Success does not come to them, they have to go towards it. Mediocrity is self-inflicted and one hopes that none of the athletes associated with the AIMS programme would be interested in mediocrity.

Preparation is the key to success. It is the meeting of preparation and opportunity which produces that marvellous thing called luck. A Texas oil billionaire once said that there were three secrets to success. First of all, a man had to work out exactly what he wanted from a certain situation. Not roughly nor vaguely, but specifically. Then he had to work out what costs need to be paid or what sacrifices would have to be made to get this result. Finally he had to be prepared to pay those costs and make those sacrifices.

Unfortunately, many athletes (from all sports) get only two out of three right. Planning is useless unless it leads to action. They should set themselves goals on a daily basis. These might relate to school, work or family commitments, as well as sport. Each training session serves a purpose in the build-up, and it is important that competitors set goals on each occasion. The goal might be quantifiable. For instance, they might be looking to run a certain distance in a particular time. But the goals could also relate to qualities such as maintaining concentration throughout a lengthy training session, or increasing the commitment to the stretching element of the warm-down.

Perhaps the most famous and most often quoted view of goal-setting comes from John Naber, an Olympic gold medalist swimmer from 1976. His progression in sport was based upon the saying, 'success leaves clues' and there was no one better than he for spotting clues. He talks of how his hero Mark Spitz motivated him to work hard by example:

> In 1972 Mark Spitz won seven gold medals, breaking seven world records. I was at home watching him, and I said to myself at the time, 'Wouldn't it be nice to be able to win a gold medal at the Olympic Games?'. So right then I had this dream of being an Olympic champion, but right about then it also became a goal.
>
> My personal best in the 100m backstroke was 59.5 seconds. Roland Matthes winning the same event for the second time went 56.3. I extrapolated his time and figured that in 1976 55.5 seconds would be the order of the day. That's what I figured I'd have to do. So I'm four seconds off the shortest backstroke event on the Olympic calendar.
>
> It's a substantial chunk. But because it's a goal now I can decisively figure out how I can attack that. I have four years to go, so it's only one second per year. Swimmers train for about ten months a year, so it's about one-tenth of a second per month. And we train six days a week and four hours a day, so it's only 1/1200th of a second every hour.
>
> Do you know how short 1/1200th of a second is? Look at my hand and blink when I click my finger. OK, it took 5/1200ths of a second for your eyes to close. For me to stand on the pool deck and say that I'm going to improve by that much in an hour is believable. I can believe in that. I can't believe I'm going to drop four seconds in four years but I can certainly believe that I can improve by 1/1200th of a second in the next hour. Couldn't you? So all of a sudden I'm moving.

John Naber went on to achieve his goal, and he clearly was a very committed individual. He was also involved in a sport which can be measured objectively and which gave him a framework to build upon. Team sport players, combat athletes and those involved in the subjective sports requiring input from judges are perhaps not quite as lucky. However, the basic premise has to be the same – that the aspiring competitor has to see himself as using every training session as a building block in his preparation.

In a similar vein, the double Olympic sprint champion Michael Johnson commented on how he made progress towards his Olympic dream, 'I traffic in a world in which fractions of a second separate success and failure, so I'd visualize the 1996 Olympics down to the millisecond. I'd crafted a decade of dreams into ambitions, refined ambitions into goals, and finally hammered goals into plans.'

The AIMS approach with international athletes has been based around the premise that the road to success is always under construction. Even reigning Olympic champions should still be striving for that little bit extra – the final winning edge that increases their chance of additional success. To this end the AIMS programme has used a variety of goal-setting regimes with several hundred athletes over the last fifteen years or so.

A word of caution on the use of goals in sport. Occasionally athletes experimenting with goal-setting for the first time suffer from the effects of a J-curve. This is the term given to a pattern in which the performance level initially goes down after an intervention, before making a dramatic improvement afterwards. Coaches should be aware of this possibility and be prepared to help the athlete through any such hiccup.

There are many different ways of employing goal-setting as a tool but the most important thing about goals is having one. How can athletes know whether they have arrived, if they do not know where they were going? Goals help in two ways: you work for them and they work for you. Clearly, the setting of goals may be an important step in any athlete's career. There are five different approaches to goal-setting utilized within the AIMS programme and they are discussed in the remainder of this chapter.

Comprehensive Goal-Setting

One approach is to use Comprehensive Goal-Setting (CGS) with individual athletes. This approach is particularly useful with young, bright athletes who have an enquiring mind. These are much more likely to want to challenge the coach and ask, 'Why are we doing this training today?' Not in the sense that they want to avoid training but more in the way they wish to understand why. For these athletes, CGS may be very useful. It is not recommended for athletes who do not have this outlook on life.

CGS is based around a premise that athletes who achieve at the highest level will need to be 'well-rounded'. They are only as strong as their weakest component. Or, to put it another way, it was not raining when Noah built the Ark. The athletes should be building their own Ark long before the unexpected happens. Accordingly they need to spend time examining the key elements of performance. Typically these have been broken down into five categories:

Technical: this relates to the skill elements of a performance
Tactical: this relates to the strategic or 'thinking' part of sport
Physical: this is based on the fitness aspect of preparation
Psychological: this refers to the mental components of sport
Environmental: this deals with lifestyle aspects associated with preparation.

The athlete starts by having an aim for a season. This is typically looking at the 'big picture'. What does he want to achieve in this year? The answers often focus on winning medals, breaking records or getting selected for championships. Following on from this starting point, they then look at goals under the headings listed above. Most competitors would have more than one goal under each heading, but this is not obligatory. These goals should complement the season's aim and should dovetail naturally into what the athlete wants to achieve.

Beneath these goals sit short-term objectives. Again, these should relate to the goals, which relate to the aim or aims. The short-term objectives would typically be updated every three or four weeks. It might be that some of these remain exactly the same for a few months; but rarely would they remain constant for an entire season. The objectives give a clear direction to the athlete and help to focus attention on the key areas of preparation.

Unfortunately, too many performers spend too much time working on their strengths and not enough time working on their limitations. The golfer who has a good long iron game but who is inconsistent at chipping will invariably spend more time hitting long irons than he will short ones. The CGS approach demands that athletes keep a balanced perspective. Obviously coaches play an important role in this area, and I have never conducted a CGS programme without the coach being involved from the outset.

Jane Flemming is an Australian heptathlete who joined the AIMS programme in 1985. The heptathlon event in athletics includes the following disciplines: 100m hurdles, shot put, high jump, 200m, long jump, javelin and finally 800m. It is the women's equivalent to the men's decathlon. The heptathlon takes place over two days and is both physically and mentally demanding. Jane is coached by Craig Hilliard who is one of the best 'teachers' I have ever worked with. He has coached Jane throughout her career – one that has been marred by serious injury.

Nevertheless, Jane has won several medals on the world stage and was ranked second in the world in 1990. She is a physically gifted performer and that has obviously helped her enormously; but she is also blessed with great mental discipline and application, and she truly maximized her performance because she has combined mental and physical preparation during her career.

A copy of Jane's CGS details from 1985 is included here (**Figure 2**). At this stage she was 21 years old and was desperate to find out just how good she could be. At the time I was a full-time sport psychologist at the Australian Institute of Sport (AIS) and was responsible for delivering psychology support services to, among others, the athletics team. The CGS is included verbatim with Jane's permission. It was developed by Jane but with assistance from Craig and some suggestions from the sport psychologist. This is typical of how the ideal relationship between coach, athlete and psychologist should work. All had something to contribute to the discussion and all believed in a model of equal expertise. Jane was the 'expert' athlete, Craig was the 'expert' coach and the psychologist's knowledge was in the field of mental preparation.

Fig 2   Comprehensive Goal-Setting: Jane Flemming, 1985

Aim

to make the 1986 Commonwealth Games in both the hurdles and heptathlon

Goals

Technical
1. Hurdles – run taller, consistently
2. High Jump – control and maintain speed in the latter part of the run-up
3. Shot Put – stay lower during and after the glide
4. 200m – improve use of arms and maintain high knee lift in last 50m
5. Long Jump – improve aspects of the take-off
6. Javelin throw – improve the use of legs in delivery and therefore increase application of force
7. 800m – work on improving the third 200m of the race

Tactical
8. In the 3-trial events, work on opening with a 'steady' attempt and then build on that
9. Enter high jump competitions at early heights and then take passes at easy heights

Physical
10. Increase explosive power
11. Increase strength endurance
12. Increase upper body strength

Mental
13. Maintain concentration during events and competition
14. Work on ignoring the presence of 'name' athletes
15. Develop ability to remain relaxed during competitions

Environmental
16. Control body weight
17. Take care of the body, in terms of rejuvenation activities, including massage, spa, sauna
18. Ensure that coaching 'eyes' are present when required

Short-term objectives

a.   Include regular sessions of motor imagery training for the technical events
b.   Get more high jumping sessions videotaped as the season approaches
c.   Go through many shot drills with dedicated throws' coach, being prepared initially to sacrifice distance for better form
d.   Use differential relaxation training tape twice a week to ensure relaxation in the arms

e. Introduce more take-off work for long jump
f. Introduce more drills for javelin that emphasize high elbow
g. Gradually build up explosive power and introduce basic bounding and plyometrics
h. Use progressive muscle relaxation tape once per week to improve general sensitivity to levels of muscular tension
i. Make the effort to find coaches and co-ordinate their attendance at sessions where specific technical assistance is required
j. Write your rejuvenation activities into your training programme
k. Adopt a sensible, rational approach to diet – ensuring that you eat enough quality items

This CGS exercise was typed and then the athlete and coach actually signed the document to give further verification that they 'owned' this plan. They were responsible for delivering it. Ultimately the athlete takes full responsibility for achieving her goals, but Jane was a relatively young athlete in a highly technical event and she certainly required assistance from Craig. Some readers might be surprised to learn that athletes write down their goals. Again, Michael Johnson suggests, 'A written goal is a contract with yourself and a constant reminder of all you still have to do. Having a record is vital: it's the first step in learning to put yourself on the hook, to being responsible to yourself.'

It is the responsibility of both the coach and the psychologist to ensure that the athlete does not become dependent upon them for support. Certainly Craig was always good at empowering Jane rather than the reverse. Unfortunately, there are some misguided coaches who do too much for the athletes, and then, when it comes to the big competition, they do not have the initiative or resources to get them through the critical moments of the challenge. In other words, the coach has killed them with kindness and made them less competitive as a result.

Some of Jane's CGS requires explanation to those readers who may not be familiar with track and field athletics. For instance, 3-trial events refer to activities such as long jump, javelin and shot put (point 8 above). Each competitor is entitled to three trials and the score achieved in her best attempt is the one that counts towards the final score. Ignoring 'name' athletes (14) refers to 'big name' athletes that Jane may have previously read about or admired and was likely to be competing against for the first time. Coaching 'eyes' (18) relates to a suggestion that sometimes she did not receive enough technical input from some of the specialist event coaches who were supposed to supervise a part of her work.

Obviously this CGS is one of hundreds of different ones used with athletes. Nevertheless, it gives an insight into the level of detail that can be applied in this regard. Casualness leads to casualties and this is to be avoided. Athletes do not want to become casualties. Interested coaches could use this CGS as a framework to see how they might map their own athlete's programme on to a world-class system.

Hierarchical Goal-Setting

Another interesting technique used in goal setting with elite performers relates to the mix of so-called *outcome, performance* and *process goals*. This is called Hierarchical Goal Setting (HGS). This approach is based upon the view that athletes should not be distracted by focusing exclusively on the outcome or result of an event. Rather, they should focus on the 'doing' part of their performance and this is known as the process of performance. Other writers have described this as developing mastery goals. Clearly all athletes and coaches are ultimately interested in the outcome of any competitive situation, but it seems that the best way to achieve a 'win' is to concentrate on the several tactical, technical and mental aspects of performance rather than simply or exclusively on the result.

A research paper (Jackson and Roberts, 1992) has highlighted the benefits of focusing on *mastery goals* (rather than outcome goals) while actually training or competing. They interviewed 200 elite athletes from different sports and asked them about their best and their worst moments in sport. One of the most positive performance states an athlete can experience is the perception of a so-called peak performance. Peak performance is the state of superior functioning that characterizes optimal sports performance. It may relate both to training and to competition experiences, and the researchers were keen to see whether any patterns existed. Would there be any common factors associated with these peak performances?

Jackson and Roberts's results suggested that peak performances were often associated with a 'mastery-oriented focus'. By comparison, worst performances seemed to coincide with an excessive concern for *outcome goals*. They defined mastery goals as factors that the athlete could control, such as the technical or tactical aspects of performance. In rowing terms, for example, this might relate to something specific about catches or length of stroke. These are specific technical or tactical aspects of the sport. An outcome focus concentrated on such aims as winning a certain medal.

Obviously there is no problem with wanting to win a medal, but the results from this research suggested that the best way to achieve this sort of outcome goal was actually to focus on mastery goals *during* the performance. If the mastery goals were achieved then the outcome goals tended to follow anyway. The trick was to focus on mastery goals while actually doing the event or task. The conclusion from the research was that this mastery focus needed to be worked on during training as well as during competition.

The authors suggested that the discipline of focusing on mastery goals did not come easily to all athletes and that training sessions provided the perfect opportunity to learn and acquire this focus. The goals may obviously change from outing to outing, but the important thing is to have at least one. In rowing it may be advisable to have an individual goal and a crew goal. In any event, the goals should be thought about and set before the start of the session. They should then be focused on during the session and, most importantly, they should be evaluated at the end of the session. If necessary, athletes should keep a log of which mastery goals have been used for each session. Of course, it may not be possible or appropriate to focus exclusively on these goals throughout a particular session. However, there should be parts or sections of the training sessions that lend themselves naturally to this focus.

Any *outcome goal* needs to be challenging and athletes should aim high in this regard. While they can set these high goals, they are somewhat hypothetical because no athlete or team are entirely in control of the outcome of any competition. They would not necessarily know how fit their opponents were, who is injured or who is in good form, and obviously these factors will ultimately have an influence on the final result. Presumably many competitors would like to be gold medalists at the Olympics, but few will ever reach these dizzy heights. So the outcome goal relates purely to the end result of a race, match or season. It is an interesting element, but it may not be too helpful when it comes to an athlete's getting out of bed at 5:30 on a cold, frosty morning. It does not offer enough specific focus for most athletes.

A *performance goal*, by comparison, is somewhat more under the control of the athlete. Such a goal is measurable and to a degree is dependent upon the efforts of the individual or team. However, even these goals are not entirely within the control of the athletes. Factors like the weather conditions and lane draws, for example, may have an influence on the level of performance. So a performance goal is rather more specific than an outcome goal, but even so it does not provide enough detailed feedback to the athlete. This is left to the process goals.

A *process goal* by definition has to be one over which the athlete can have complete control. It should be something that can be truly described as being entirely within the control of the athlete. No one else can influence this type of goal, and it is somewhat akin to the short-term objectives mentioned within the section on CGS. Athletes should focus on achieving the process goals and if they can get a tick in each of the boxes against this list, then they are much more likely to get a tick against the performance goal box, and if they get a tick against this box, they are much more likely to get a tick against the outcome goal box. Therefore most of the attention and focus should be at the process end, and then the outcome will take care of itself.

If, by comparison, the athlete is obsessed by focusing on a solitary outcome goal, such as, 'Gold, gold, gold', or 'Win, win, win', he or she is much more likely to make the mistake of being distracted from dealing with the all-important job at hand. Hence a key component of the AIMS programme is to encourage athletes to focus on process goals. This does not mean that they are not interested in winning! The *Gold Minds* are very keen on winning, but they know that the best way of achieving this is to focus on the smaller details of process goals.

Three examples from the 1996 British rowing team are included here by way of demonstrating that even crews and athletes within the same sport may have quite different views on the same topic at the same time of the year (**Figures 3 to 5**). Each crew was undergoing a roughly similar conditioning programme because the calendar year dictates that there is a certain volume of work to be completed during the spring. However, a close examination of the three different HGS responses shows a marked difference in emphasis from one crew to another. This is entirely appropriate, of course.

As the Olympics got closer, so the number of process goals was reduced. At a training camp in France in June, the number went down to six, and in the Olympic village itself (four weeks later) it was reduced further to three. The thinking behind this approach is that as the pressure mounts, athletes are less likely to be able to focus on multiple goals and accordingly we work together to identify those elements which are absolutely mission-critical. To date, this approach has been fairly successful and the athletes welcome this narrowing of attention at this particularly stressful stage.

Fig 3 Men's Eight: Goal-setting, April 1996

Outcome goal

Win medal

Performance goal

5 min 18 sec

Process goals

- Uniformity of technique – rhythm and remembering how the power is produced
- Notion of consistency and rhythm – make it a habit (second nature)
- Improve the focus – knowing when to switch on and off
- Training to the best physiological effect
- Enjoying the training and preparation
- Have a general tolerance of each other
- Do daily goal setting – not necessarily coach-led
- Work towards improving mental skills aspect
- Experiment with being able to use more aggression in training pieces
- Be prepared to accept internal crew feedback: free sharing of opinions
- Improve attitude towards flexibility
- Monitor the levels of 'pressure' within the crew
- Build the crew's confidence level – no fear
- Develop communication skills using the cox as the focus
- Start the process of looking at village skills

- Work on lifestyle skills – punctuality as an example
- Develop fast economical start
- Improve mental attitude for each session
- Evolution of good crew spirit
- Be able to evaluate your own performance
- Management of rest and recovery
- Management of injury and illness

Fig 4   Men's Lightweight Four: Goal-setting, April 1996

Outcome goal

Win a Gold medal in Atlanta

Performance goals

5:47
Win medals at other regattas during season

Process goals

- Have a quick, sharp, sweet catch
- Work on finish timing and having the same length
- Practice race pace and have an emphasis on start speed (but do not overcook it)
- All 'moves' done as one
- Maintain strength improvements
- Learn the race plan and have the faith to follow it to the bitter end
- Be responsible for your own bodyweight and also assist your crew mates without putting pressure on them
- Don't put excessive pressure on to win every race during the season
- Train as a crew more often
- Paddle well consistently – make it a habit
- Make good use of the 'switch' – be able to tune in quickly because you've practised it in training
- Be videotaped more often and get to see the film afterwards
- Eat well and control weight – arrange session with the nutritionist
- Improve crew unity – remembering the difference between task and social cohesion
- Improve the quality and quantity of communication between the crew

Fig 5   Men's Coxless Four: Goal-setting, April 1996

Outcome goal

Gold medal in Atlanta

Performance goal

5:45

Process goals

- Work specifically on last 4 weeks
- Row 'long' – effective length, strong position, effective ends of strokes
- Use each race and each day effectively – have specific aims and live in present tense
- Extra commitment to the first half of the race
- Experiment with the best way of maximizing the last 30 strokes
- Work towards race fitness – intensity of each piece or outing
- Discard the mental baggage – special attention to the media and the 'switch'
- Work towards all crew members having the same focus
- Maintain healthy outlook and see rowing as part of life
- Improve communications within crew – try not to irritate others
- Improve attitude towards flexibility work
- Recommit to mental skills work
- Ensure an effective management of rest and recovery

It may clearly be seen that there are significant differences between the crews and yet there are also similarities. As the Olympic Games get closer, then the number of process goals should diminish and/or some of the goals may need refining or adjusting. The emphasis remains on the process goals at this late stage of the preparation and, if anything, the athletes need to retain this focus even more as the Olympics approach.

A former colleague at the AIS in Canberra, Jeff Bond, had a great deal of success using this approach with the Wimbledon tennis champion Pat Cash. Pat is a very gifted tennis player who won Wimbledon in 1987 and was highly focused on living in the 'present tense' and on process goals. His press interviews in the euphoric aftermath of victory clearly showed that he was concentrating on things such as foot movement or the toss-up for the serve, especially at critical stages in his matches. He took care of the process goals – got ticks against all or most of these – and then the outcome took care of itself.

The British women's hockey team took a similar approach in their build-up to the Atlanta Games. As a team they were clearly motivated towards winning an Olympic medal, but they realized that if they focused narrowly on the outcome alone they would forget to take care of all of the processes required for success. In a group meeting at Bisham Abbey in May 1996 they identified the following as a list of process goals they would need to focus on during the intervening eight weeks of preparation. Again, it is evident that these goals are sport-specific and some of the subtleties are lost if one is not a hockey aficionado. Nevertheless, it is apparent that this group of highly motivated performers adopted a pragmatic approach to their final preparation, and once again, it may be seen that the players developed these goals for and by themselves.

GB Women's Hockey Team 1996: Group Process Goals

- Maintain consistent routines in warm-ups for matches
- Plan strategies for dealing with distractions
- Re short corners – 25 per cent conversion rate from attacking situations and 15 per cent from defending situations
- Be prepared to accept and act upon constructive feedback from colleagues and management
- Quality training in regional sessions – concentrate on basic and relevant skills
- Plan for productive use of time while in village
- Develop sensitivity towards individuals especially in tournament situation
- Value people's personal space
- Be honest and yet sensitive
- Utilize effective goal setting throughout the build-up
- Control the controllables
- Create a 'presence' on and off the pitch
- In pre-tournament phase (trip to North Carolina) develop a positive balance
- Narrow focus on team and individual goals
- Have task-oriented thoughts
- Live in the present tense
- Develop an even more positive mental attitude
- Maintain a correct diet (especially in village)
- Maintain tolerance of each other as the pressure mounts
- Improve mental attitude for each training session
- Maintain focus on goals and don't waste energy on uncontrollables
- Develop ability to stay in control especially under pressure
- Manage indifferent umpiring if faced with any during Olympics and build-up

This list was subsequently reduced as the Games approached and players focused on the key elements of success. Feedback from the players suggested that this was most important, especially when faced with various difficult situations in Atlanta.

Aiming for Success

During 1990 the British Olympic Association formed a Psychology Steering Group made up of Richard Butler, Lew Hardy and myself. I learned a good deal from these two pioneers and certainly Richard's contributions in relation to goal-setting were substantial. In particular, he introduced the concept of Construct Theory and his application of it in the form of Performance Profiling (see Butler, 1997). The AIMS programme modified Richard's approach slightly and incorporated his work in the use of 'dartboards' or 'spiders' webs' with a number of teams and individuals from 1991 onwards. There are parallels between process goals and the 'spokes' on the dartboards.

In each instance the psychologist leads the competitor through a couple of sessions in which he describes which 'constructs' are important when it comes to producing a good performance or a good preparation for a competition. Typically, this would include a list of ten to twenty items. Then a coach might get involved and help the athlete to refine the list down to a key twelve. These items could be described as the major components of any process goals.

Having identified the relevant 'spokes', the competitor would train for a week, concentrating on these features. On a Sunday evening, he would sit down and review progress against these specific items. Subjectively, a score out of ten would be assigned to each spoke. The athlete would then compare all of the scores he had given himself, and would focus especially hard on the weaker scores during the coming week. It is as if the dartboards were offering him some clues as to where to put the relative effort.

Many athletes actually join the several dots on the constructs together and go to the trouble of shading in the resultant shape on the dartboard. Clearly, this act itself is never going to make any athlete a champion. Rather it is the thought processes that accompany this which are of great importance. On the one hand the athlete is accepting ownership of his current situation on a week-by-week basis, and on the other he is reminding himself of the need to search constantly for continuous improvement in his preparation.

In other words, the athlete has bought himself into the process of setting benchmarks for himself, measuring himself against them and then accepting ownership of the dozen constructs. Ultimately it is the competitor who will have to compete in the Olympic arena and he will need to be able to face any number of adversities. Therefore it is the athlete who should accept responsibility for making progress in each of the important 'spokes'. One of the keys to the entire 'dartboarding' exercise is that the athletes make an important contribution to the process. They should thus have a substantial say in choosing the key constructs. As Danny Everett, Olympic gold medalist, put it: 'You have to be patient and accomplish your goals. Don't try to accomplish other people's goals... you need to take small steps one at a time and not big strides to fulfil other people's expectations.'

There has also been some success in this area in asking both athletes and their coaches to fill in these dartboards. In other words, the athlete rates himself (marks out of ten) against the twelve items, and then the coach also gives an assessment of how well he thinks the athlete has performed in these areas. Some of the resultant discussions concerning the relative differences have led to free and frank exchanges of opinions. But in most cases these have been important sessions in which the quality of communication between the coach and the athlete has improved immeasurably.

The four examples included here again show some of the marked differences between, for example, racing drivers, hockey players and track and field athletes (**Figures 6 to 9**). These are certainly highly sport-specific but they also reflect a high degree of individualism within each performer. It is also worth noting the dartboard from Jane Flemming. This was developed some six years after the CGS and shows some of the changes involved in a maturing athlete. Between the CGS and the dartboard, Jane had won two Commonwealth gold medals, one Commonwealth silver, one World Student Games bronze and had been ranked number two in the world. She had certainly achieved at the highest level, and accordingly some of her key areas of focus had changed.

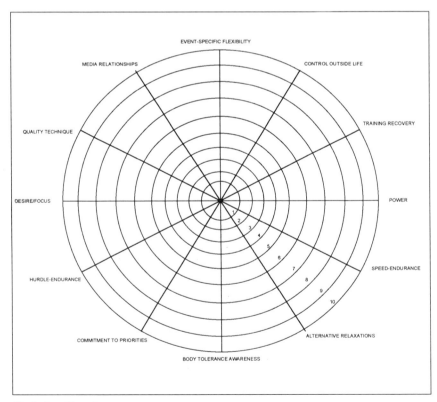

Fig 6   Jane Flemming

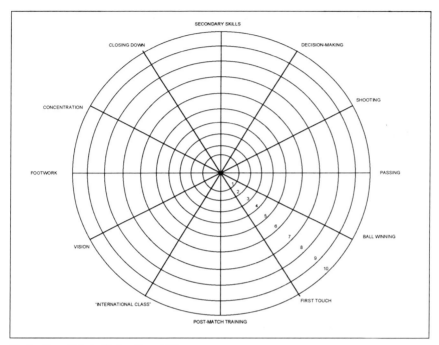

Fig 7 Great Britain Hockey Team 1992

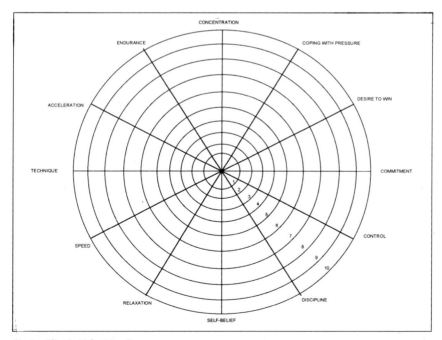

Fig 8 Elite British 400m Runner

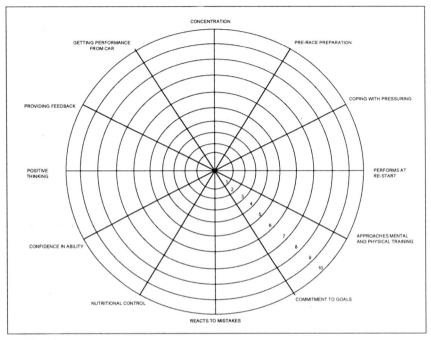

Fig 9   Professional Formula 3 Racing Driver

Goal-Setting for Training Sessions

> If I do not practise one day, I know it. If I do not practise the next, the orchestra knows it. If I do not practise the third day, the whole world knows it.
>
> *Ignace Paderewski, world-renowned concert pianist*

> As for my forearms, nature gave me part of them, but the other part I found in the gym one day, right next to the weight machine. It's amazing what you might find if you work out a little.
>
> *Martina Navratilova, world-class tennis player*

While techniques such as CGS, HGS and the dartboards are helpful for giving athletes and coaches a sense of the big picture, there is still a need to have athletes taking care of the smaller elements of preparation. As we stated earlier, planning is useless unless it is actually transformed into work. Accordingly, athletes should set themselves goals for each training session.

It is important that these goals are set before the start of a given training session and then evaluated once the session is over. This is the key to purposeful and effective preparation. Elite athletes would typically go through a great many training sessions each year and most coaches would agree that if it were possible to make each one of these 1 per cent more effective, then the net gain over an entire season would be significant.

Greg Searle weight training prior to the 1996 Olympic Games.

In some sports athletes tend to spend a lot more time training than competing, and it is vital that they get the most out of it. It should never get to the stage when they simply go through the motions of another work-out. Once the coach has explained the major points of the workload for a session, the athlete should then start to get his or her mind in gear and focus on one or two key elements for that session. Perhaps while they are going through the first part of their warm-up, they could set themselves a target for the rest of the work-out.

Figure 10 is a sample page of what a training diary for a young athlete might look like. The AIMS programme has previously used it with British and Australian Olympians. The forms were originally developed for the Australian women's hockey team in 1986. In 1988 they became Olympic champions for the first time. For each session the athlete gets a chance to set two goals. At the end of the session, she can then review herself on a scale of 1 to 10 and make any comments that seem relevant. These comments might help to set targets for the next day's training.

Fig 10   Australian Women's Hockey Squad 1986 Training Evaluation Sheet

Date .... Nature or content of session:

Rate on a five-point scale:

1 = the pits!
2 = below average
3 = average
4 = above average
5 = very good

Pre-training 'appetite'	1 2 3 4 5
'Tuning-in' ability	1 2 3 4 5
Quality of warm-up	1 2 3 4 5
Concentration capacity	1 2 3 4 5
Quality of warm-down	1 2 3 4 5
Feeling after training	1 2 3 4 5

Which two aspects of the session were you most happy with?

1.
2.

Which features of the session were you least happy with?

1.
2.

Any other general comments?

After using this type of system for a while, any competitor should be able to reflect on previous training sessions to see 'where he's come from' over the weeks or months. This should help to lead to an enhanced self-image and contribute to the Success Cycle.

In addition, by adopting this approach the athlete is learning about how the CGS or HGS works in an applied setting. There is nothing worse than going through an in-depth goal-setting exercise for the entire season if the resulting document is then confined to the coach's drawer and not referred to again. By using a form of daily goal setting I am convinced that the athlete begins to see the link between theory and practice, and this again allows him to take ownership of the situation.

Steve Redgrave has blood taken from his ear to monitor training, while partner Matthew Pinsent awaits his turn.

Professionalism Goals

Another important area in which goals may be helpful is in the preparation for international touring or competition. While employed at the AIS in Canberra, I worked quite extensively with young Australians from many sports who toured the world in search of top-class competitive experience. These athletes were quite used to employing goal-setting in the sense of CGS or HGS. It seemed only natural to develop a system which would allow them to keep a quality focus while encountering new and different experiences. It was hoped that this would allow them to maximize the benefit from any tours and stand them in good stead for subsequent world championships or Olympic Games. Not surprisingly, this work has continued with many British competitors.

An example has been included of some work completed with the AIS netball squad which toured the Caribbean in 1986. Some notes on touring skills, as well as some examples of the professionalism goals which were established by the players have been included. The average age of this group was about 21 and for many of them this was their first overseas tour. Coincidentally, six or seven of these players later went on to be world champions with the Australian national team.

Caribbean Preparation – 1986

Some factors for you to consider on this tour are :
1. Normality of eating habits. Temptation to overeat or eat many different foods. Be especially careful after matches.
2. Effects of boredom. Tendency to overeat or go walking around shopping centres and spend too much time on your feet. This tour has a tough schedule.
3. Preparation for relative inactivity during bus trips. Have some diversions available such as books or a Walkman.
4. Control of excitement. Keeping things in proportion, especially if it's your first time overseas.
5. Accelerated and accumulated fatigue. Touring athletes often talk of the fatigue creeping up on them. Make good use of 'semi-sleep' and dozing. This is particularly important when you consider that you have major matches right at the end of the tour.
6. As foreigners on tour you will need to use each other as a resource. You are very much the 'privileged visitors' in the Caribbean. You will be exposed to different lifestyles, and some standards of living that might surprise you. You will react as individuals. Respect the individual differences within the group. People will have fluctuations in mood during any tour.
7. Refer back to your performance and professionalism goals at different times during the tour. This will help you to retain your focus.

The players then completed a form before departure which listed their two performance goals and two professionalism goals. The performance goals related to things they did on the court, while the professionalism ones related to things they did off the court. A professionalism goal was likely to be based around some aspect of self-management which could impact negatively on netball performance. Each player had to announce her goals to the group and each had to keep a log of how she measured against these stated goals. Most of these relatively inexperienced players could come up with several netball-specific goals, but they often found the off-court goals a little more difficult. However, with some prompting they produced a list which included the following;

1. To eat only nutritious food while on road trips.
2. I will try hard to get on with all other athletes on tour.
3. Use my Walkman for recreation and relaxation on long trips during the tour.
4. Ensure that I don't react to suspect umpiring in a negative way.
5. Even when I know we're playing against weaker opponents, I'll ensure that my warm-up is consistently thorough.
6. Do some 'recreational' knitting everyday.
7. Make sure I get some day-time sleep everyday.
8. I will keep reasonable hours during the trip and be aware of my room-mate's wishes.
9. Make sure I do my mental rehearsal at least once a day.
10. I won't overeat at breakfast, even if they lay on 'the works'.
11. I will try to be a supportive member of the squad, even when I'm a reserve and not getting much court time.
12. I won't drink any booze until the last night!

Another example of goal-setting for trips or camps comes from the British women's rowing team in 1996. Before a training camp in Spain in February they had identified the critical success factors which they viewed as being the cornerstone of success. Before they left, they were presented with the following memorandum:

> In relation to the items identified by you as being important, your training camp can be used very effectively to start the ball rolling. In order to look at critical factors, you should:
> Set yourself two goals every day. These could focus on off- and on-water issues and they should remind you of the session that took place in London last week. Having set those goals then ensure that you achieve those goals and devote at least some of your energies to attaining them. Make a note on a daily basis as to how well you achieved those goals.
> In addition, you should make a daily note of at least two things that have gone well during that day. If there are more, then write those down as well. When you return from the camp we will review the process to see what progress has been made.

In this instance goal-setting is being combined with confidence building.

The performers were being asked to set goals, work to attain them, and also record a log of things that had gone well. The requirement to set on- and off-water goals was obviously the same as the performance and professionalism goals used with the young netballers ten years before.

In summary, it is important to encourage athletes to make commitments to goals. A self-motivated athlete makes commitments while ordinary performers simply make promises. Coaches should not be interested in promises because these are little better than New Year resolutions – they are easily forgotten and more easily broken. By comparison, a written commitment or pledge is much more likely to be adhered to. Athletes with goals succeed because they know where they are going. If you do not know where you are supposed to be going, how can you expect to get there? There is a good analogy of boats with or without rudders. If a boat has no rudder (or an athlete has no goals) it is at the vagaries of the wind and tide. It may end up in a good port, but probably not. An athlete's goals are like his or her rudder. You can make your way on to the medal rostrum without them, but it certainly becomes a risky business. Many people dream of winning medals, but only a few stay awake and win them. Goal-setting is an important element in athletes staying awake and working effectively to achieve their potential. Many have the will to win but only the *Gold Minds* have the will to prepare to win.

CHAPTER TWO

Pre-Competition Arousal

Just lying or sitting quietly, sometimes closing my eyes and imagining myself playing well all helped me psych myself up. I didn't try to stop myself being nervous before a match. Being nervous helped me concentrate and blend into the competitive atmosphere. I would be worried if I wasn't nervous before a match.

Evonne Goolagong Cawley, Australian tennis player

The psych wasn't there. I wasn't mentally prepared... It just wasn't my day. It wasn't my race.

Tom Fleming, world-class marathoner, on dropping out of the Boston Marathon

The only limitations are mental: you can do anything you want, and the guy who thinks most positively will win.

Daley Thompson, double Olympic decathlon champion

A sport psychologist has many roles to play in the preparation of athletes, and time has shown that the number of roles and services is constantly increasing. However, the general area of immediate pre-competition preparation remains a central theme for the applied sport psychologist. It certainly holds a special place within the AIMS programme, and the level of sophistication characterizing this aspect is increasing at a dramatic rate.

There is no set figure as to how long pre-event preparation should last. The AIMS programme normally refers to a potential time span of anything from a week to one second before the gun. Several common reactions have been identified during the period of pre-event preparation, and these appear to be consistent across all groups or levels. This chapter will focus on the generalizations concerning preparation; the Appendix deals with some of the specific techniques.

As competition time approaches, athletes often show signs of reacting to stress. The reasons for this are manifold, but the responses are often quite predictable. Experience with athletes at all levels suggests that the three most common responses are:

- A chronic lack of self-confidence
- Increased levels of residual tension
- Reduced levels of patience and tolerance.

These responses are predictable and understandable, but they also have to be managed if the athlete is to fulfil his or her potential. Providing that the self-confidence issue is not too severe, it can be a relatively minor problem because most athletes are experiencing the same sort of feelings.

Nearly all athletes consider (if only momentarily) the problems of their recent performances or ponder over their recent training performances.

In 1996 Steve Redgrave and Matthew Pinsent famously won the coxless pairs event at the Atlanta Games. It was Redgrave's fourth gold and Pinsent's second. They had been undefeated in their event since 1992 – a winning streak of fifty-nine races. Not surprisingly, they were described as favourites for the gold medal. However, in the press conference following their victory Pinsent alluded to the pressures the pair were under during the build-up to the event. He said,

> It has been pretty tough just hanging around in the hotel for the last two days. The last few days have been extremely tense, and we have been very nervous. This morning we woke up to the news of the terrorist bomb, which is not the ideal news to hear, but we had to blank it out and get on with the race. We had a chat with our coach, and we sorted out a few things in our heads, so this morning when we went to the line we felt slightly better.

This pair of athletes were perhaps two of the hottest favourites in Olympic rowing history, with an impressive string of results behind them. Yet they were still highly nervous in those last few days before their final.

Similarly, in the press conference after the 200m track event final Michael Johnson (gold medal) and Frank Fredericks (silver) also commented on the pressure associated with competing at this level. Johnson went for, and achieved, a unique double of winning the gold in both the 200m and the 400m event. He commented:

> I have never felt pressure like this in my life. Every time I opened a newspaper or a magazine there was something about this double. People were calling to try to take the pressure off and just adding more pressure. I was scared out there but I run well when I am scared. I love pressure. You have to embrace pressure, to understand it, to draw it in, to make it your own and use it to your advantage. Pressure is nothing more than the shadow of great opportunity. The pressure builds and builds until the defining moment, and that is the time I crave.

Fredericks said, 'I don't like the pressure, I can't handle it. I realized that in the 100m final. There was too much pressure and it was very emotional for me.'

The British track star Brendan Foster once commented that in the weeks leading up to major championships he would often ask himself whether the balance between speed and endurance training had been right, and he would still worry even if he was in great form.

Nine-times Olympic champion Carl Lewis has competed in four Olympic Games and has witnessed some of the things that tend to affect first time Olympians. He says,

> One of the biggest problems for some athletes is that they put too much emphasis on trying to make everything perfect. Before a race they wonder if they warmed up too much or not enough. At meals they are worried that they are eating too much, but the last thing they want to do is be short of

energy. At night they are talking about getting too much sleep or not enough. It is easy to worry about things that are not going to make a big difference.

Experienced athletes seem to be able to forget about these negative thoughts once the event begins. However, the second aspect of pre-competition preparation, residual tension, can be a major cause of concern. If the level of physical tension goes unchecked, it can be a significant predictor of under achievement in elite sport. When an athlete becomes anxious he generates tension and, in time, this may accumulate to disruptive levels.

When the amount of stress becomes too high an individual's functioning may be affected on four levels:

Cognitive: a dysfunctional system of thinking is established. In other words, the athlete tends to think the worst and ignore the positive. He may take a negative view about his ability or previous achievements, and over-generalize about negative experiences. One bad performance or training session is suddenly translated into the self-belief that the athlete is not very good. I have seen experienced Olympians arrive at unrealistically pessimistic conclusions based upon their performances in an earlier, minor competition. It is almost as if the dysfunctional thinking makes them forget all of their previous successes in the sport. The extent of this problem cannot be overrestimated, especially as the day of a key event approaches.

Physiological: when an athlete (but the same is true of any organism) perceives a threat, he generally prepares for emergency action by increasing his level of arousal in order to be capable of reacting appropriately. However, if the arousal level is heightened too much then the body is thrown out of its normal homeostatic state, and this may interfere with performance. The most common physiological stress responses in performers tend to relate to increased gastrointestinal activity, increased skin response (sweating), increased levels of muscular tension, increased heart rate and an elevated respiration rate.

Behavioural: in elite athletes the most common behavioural response to stress is that of avoidance. I have worked with several who have gone to extraordinary lengths to ensure that they do not have to compete when they are slightly below their highest level. It often seems as if their reaction to stress is not to put themselves to the test and this may be frustrating for coaches, friends and families.

The former Olympic champion Sally Gunnell once commented that she was so nervous before her Olympic final in Barcelona in 1992 that she hoped that a helicopter might suddenly appear and whisk her away, so that she would not have to compete. A few minutes afterwards she was crowned as Olympic champion and is obviously now glad that no helicopter did arrive to 'rescue' her. Nevertheless, this anecdote goes to exemplify some of the potentially irrational behaviours considered by elite performers when they are under extreme pressure.

Affective: in the period leading up to major championships the most common affective changes seem to relate to such feelings as apprehension, worry, guilt, fear, aggression and irritability. I have been around perfectly healthy, finely-tuned athletes at times of great perceived stress and some of their behaviours resemble those of Dr Jekyll and Mr Hyde. They may change their way of reacting very dramatically and quickly. This pattern of behaviour can be confusing for the coaches.

As mentioned earlier in this chapter, there may often be problems with irritability and mood swings. Trivial incidents may suddenly have significant consequences for athletes. In the Atlanta Olympic Games, for example, one British rower came close to physically assaulting a member of the American military over a fairly innocuous comment made by the soldier who was driving a bus. The athlete was physically restrained by others before he was able to do anything untoward, but it serves as a good example as to how people apparently change when under pressure. The athlete concerned is 'normally' gentle, reasonable and rational. But under the pressure of the Games he was then far from rational.

Arousal and Performance

There has been a great deal written on the relationship between arousal and performance and some of it is contradictory. When one considers the four levels of stress response outlined earlier in this chapter, it is hard to imagine how people could consider that arousal or stress is helpful to performance. However, the issue is complex and it is not helped by some confusion in the literature concerning the terminology. Words are often used interchangeably. In simple terms, cognitive anxiety may be viewed as the mental element of anxiety caused by negative expectations; whereas somatic anxiety is the physiological element of anxiety related to autonomic arousal.

This differentiation has been helpful in the development of a 'matching hypothesis' which suggests that unwanted cognitive anxiety should be controlled or reduced with a cognitive relaxation technique, while physical symptoms might respond better if a somatic relaxation technique were employed. This is a sensible, common-sense approach, and yet there have been at least five or six AIMS athletes who have won gold medals at the Olympics, and for whom the exact opposite of the matching hypothesis is true. Nothing is ever clear cut.

Perhaps the most famous theory for explaining behaviour under a variety of arousal conditions is known as the 'inverted-U' or Yerkes–Dodson law. The theory suggests that performance increases in proportion to increases in arousal up to a certain limit. Beyond this there

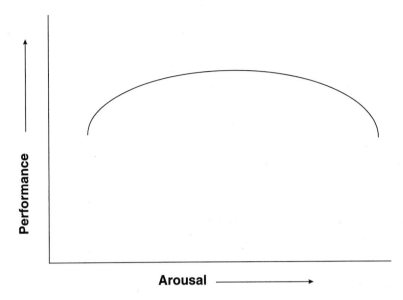

Fig 11.

is a performance decrement where things start to go wrong. **Figure 11** shows this proposed relationship.

The inverted-U shape demonstrates that it is possible for an athlete to perform below his best because he is over-aroused, just as he may perform badly because he is under-aroused. The area where top-class performances are going to occur is within the Zone of Optimal Functioning or ZOF. This 'corridor' of tolerance on either side of the optimal level of arousal is the ZOF, or what some athletes describe as being 'in the zone'. In this respect the AIMS programme tries to give athletes control over their own level of arousal so that they may move freely along the horizontal axis of **Figure 11**.

In addition, it is worth noting that advocates of Cusp Catastrophe theory (see Fazey and Hardy 1988, for example) would also question the overall shape of the graph. They might conclude that the 'drop off' in performance once the ideal 'psych' level has been passed is far more dramatic. They might also suggest that cognitive anxiety does not always have a negative effect on performance. Some performers may perform at their best despite experiencing high levels of cognitive anxiety. One of the AIMS gold medalists sat crying only hours before his gold-medal performance. He was a very frightened young man who was full of self-doubt and could have been described as a prime candidate for a little catastrophe theory. History shows that he was able to channel this high level of cognitive anxiety into a 'focused', awe-inspiring performance and he confessed afterwards that, despite the fear, he felt able to concentrate better than ever before.

Similarly, Silken Laumann, a great Canadian oarswoman, has commented, 'I've had to learn to consider the nervousness as something positive. The tension means you're ready and you care. A great coach knows that the adrenaline is potentially useful and works with the athlete to channel it, not to shut it down. So I pay attention to my breathing and visualize the first five or six strokes.'

In any event, the views of the catastrophe theorists only further emphasize the need for the athlete to be in control of both somatic and cognitive arousal levels.

On some occasions the athlete may require more arousal and on other occasions less. The significant issue is that the athletes need to acquire techniques which will allow them to regulate their own levels. This category of mental skills are generally known as self-regulation techniques and several of them are outlined in the Appendix. These represent some of those that I have found to be the most useful. But, by themselves, the techniques are useless.

Self-regulation skills are used for both calming and energizing individuals. There are occasions when athletes have to increase arousal, and other times when they need to reduce it. The significant aspect of the AIMS programme is that it gives athletes the opportunity to move themselves in either direction. Other authors have often stressed only the need to examine relaxation techniques; but they have tended to minimize the important role played by energizing techniques. My experience has shown that while some 80 per cent of the skills are for calming athletes, there are another 20 per cent that are vital for energizing purposes.

The initial step required before using any of the techniques (for either relaxing or energizing) is one of self-monitoring. Athletes are taught to identify the physical symptoms associated with excessive levels of arousal. They have to develop a 'street-sense' of their own bodies and be able to react accordingly in the pre-event period. The emphasis is on self-awareness. Athletes are taught to find out which of the bodily systems react most for them under pressure (perhaps the clue is heart rate or muscular tension), and then become in tune with how minor variations within this system influence performance. In other words, they learn to find out where they are along the horizontal axis of **Figure 11** at any time.

Being able to monitor the ways in which the body responds to pressure is a distinct advantage in sport. But the bodily systems represent only half of the picture. Clearly the brain is important as well. When I see an athlete getting too worked up or too worried I often say, 'Don't lose your head – it's the best part of your body.' Athletes who have trouble monitoring both physical and mental states pre-competition are often encouraged to use a grid to describe pictorially how they are feeling. Some authors prefer to use questionnaires, but the AIMS programme uses a simple grid because it is less intrusive and this is important when the athlete is so close to competition time.

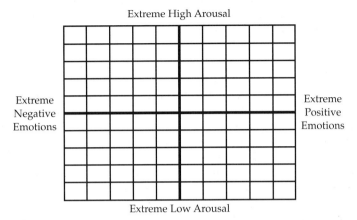

Fig 12.

The athlete quite simply places an 'X' in any box, representing where he sits on the two dimensions: arousal and emotions. This grid exercise may be used to show that high arousal does not always lead to negative emotions and vice versa. The grid can offer clues as to how people should prepare for big events.

After having assessed the level of pre-event arousal, the next stage is to have a skill or skills that allows the athlete to modify his arousal level as seems appropriate at that time.

Waldemar Cierpinski, East Germany's two-time Olympic marathon champion, once claimed that his mental preparation was the key to his success in major races. He managed to keep his pulse down to less than forty beats per minute as he stood on the starting line for each of those marathons, and this is testimony as to how composed he was in the under pressure. Athletes following the AIMS programme are normally taught a variety of self-regulation skills to give them the same control as Cierpinski, and many of them have applied these skills in that same Olympic cauldron.

The next problem that faces the coach or the athlete is that of choosing an appropriate technique to learn. All self-regulation skills have to be learned just as any other skill does, and experience has shown that there are three things that have to be kept in mind before embarking on any skill-learning programme:

- Athletes vary in the speed at which they learn to self-regulate
- Athletes must be motivated to want to learn these techniques
- Athletes have to invest time and effort if they are to derive benefit from these exercises.

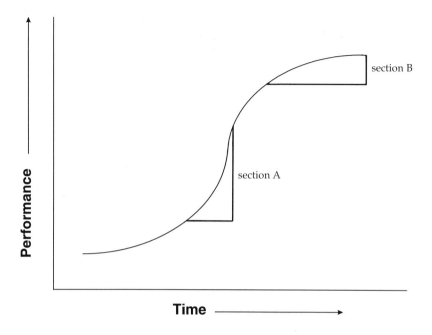

Fig 13

Athletes setting out on the AIMS programme for the first time are made aware of these 'laws' before the teaching gets under way. They respond at a much faster rate if they have such details explained to them. **Figure 13** is also used to illustrate the likely avenue of progress for each athlete. Many athletes respond well to this approach because they see it as a challenge. It is almost as if they were determined to outdo others who have previously set out to learn the skills.

Figure 13 is the classical description of the relationship between skill learning and the amount of time and effort required to acquire these skills. In section A of the curve, things tend to go along well, with skill gains being made for relatively little time and effort. It seems as if progress can be made easily. Virtually everyone can move along the curve quickly at this stage. However, during section B the rate of progress slows and not all seem to be able to improve during this phase. It is almost as if, when they are faced with the plateau of skill learning, they somehow reduce their efforts.

However, the small gains made during this phase are the vital ones because not everyone gets up to this level. I tend to explain to athletes that not all individuals seem capable of reaching the top of the skill learning curve. So, just as they have probably spent many hours practising the physical skills of their chosen sport, they will have to invest time and effort to acquire these new psychological elements. This typically produces a competitive response from many of the elite performers. They accept that there are going to be lulls in their progress and are willing to persevere when these arise. Often this attitude allows them to go on and develop a wide array of self-regulation skills because they work hard during the plateau phase.

Modifying Levels of Pre-Event Arousal

When it comes to altering the level of pre-event arousal there are basically two options: the athlete needs to calm down or to be energized. Within these two categories there are two types of technique; one is somatic or physical and the other is cognitive or 'of the brain'.

Calming Techniques

BREATHING DRILLS

> I like to use breathing drills in those vital last minutes before the gun. I find that they focus my mind on the job in hand. It's as if I am doing a mental warm-up before the race and this makes me think clearer in the pressure situations.
>
> *Don Wright, Olympic high hurdler*

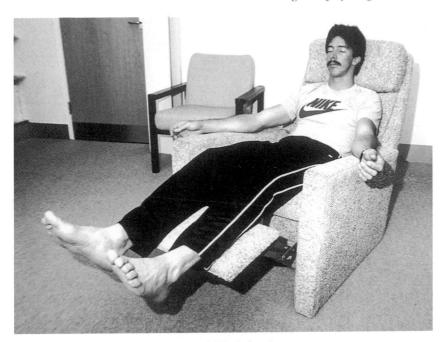

Olympic high hurdler Don Wright using Modal Ten Relaxation.

The most appropriate physical way of reducing pre-event arousal is to use one or more breathing drills. Some of the more common methods are described in the Appendix. They may all be used relatively briefly to good effect while at the competition site. Many authors have emphasized the importance of learning somatic relaxation skills, in the vague hope that by relaxing the body while away from the competition site, the athlete will somehow perform at a higher level when he does get to the venue.

Originally, I also recommended this approach. However, experience has shown that, while the somatic relaxation techniques are useful for reducing residual tension away from the venue (for instance, using progressive muscle relaxation on the morning of a big afternoon race), they are relatively ineffective if used in the last hour or so before a competition.

Many of the somatic strategies simply take too long to complete. This is the major reason for the heavy emphasis on acquiring a variety of breathing techniques within the AIMS programme. These techniques are used only in a relaxation context. It is possible to use short, sharp breaths

1. Stand comfortably with your feet shoulder distance apart and your knees slightly flexed.

2. Consciously relax your neck, arm and shoulder muscles. Smile slightly to reduce the tension in your jaw.

3. Focus on the movement of your abdominal muscles. Notice your stomach muscles tightening and relaxing.

Inhalation

4. Take a slow, deep breath using the diaphragm. Notice you are extending your stomach.

5. Consciously maintain the relaxation in your chest and shoulders. There should be minimal chest movement and absolutely no hunching or raising of the shoulders.

6. Exhale slowly. Let yourself go. Feel yourself get heavier as all your muscles relax.

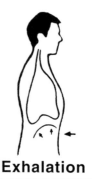

Exhalation

Fig 14   Centering.

as an energizing tool, but I have found little success with that approach and now firmly advise against it. The use of one or more of the five breathing techniques described in the Appendix is recommended.

Each technique may be best learned in a quiet, comfortable setting, but eventually they have to be applied in the real world of competition or training. Typically, the progression would be to use the drills first at home, then in training and then immediately before competition.

I enjoy watching a successful AIMS athlete using a technique, such as centering, while standing on the starting line before a race (*see* Fig 14). It indicates that the athlete is sensitive to his body's reactions and that he has good control over his arousal level. But, like most skills exhibited by the elite athlete, he makes them look easy. The reality of the situation is that the breathing technique has been practised on numerous occasions in a variety of environments before the athlete could correctly be described as having an automatic skill.

Centering is a breathing technique originally developed about two thousand years ago by Tibetan monks. Today it is arguably the world's most commonly used mental-training device. Most eastern European athletes were taught this technique in the days when state-run systems were in operation. Centering is essentially a technique that can help an athlete to reduce tension before a competition. It gives the athlete control over his body and allows him to dictate the level of pre-event arousal. Athletes who take the time to learn centering can keep the technique as a weapon in their armoury. They do not have to use the skill every time they compete, but they know that it is there if they need it. This can be a great confidence booster.

If athletes practise centering in front of a mirror for about one minute a day for a fortnight, they acquire the skill and then have virtually got it for life. One or two minutes' practice per week will allow them to stay in touch with the exercise, and then they can use it at any time before or during an event. It would be used whenever they felt that their nervous-ness was just a little too high and they wanted to gain control. Because centering is so easy to do and can be performed so briefly it is of use to all sportsmen and women. Another strength of this technique is that athletes can use it without other people noticing that it is being utilized. By learning a skill such as centering the AIMS athlete is helping to mini-mize the risk of 'choking' on the big day. It is a small investment for such a potentially big reward, and athletes of all standards from all sports can benefit from its use.

IMAGERY DRILLS

The second category of calming techniques is cognitive relaxation and is based around imagining various relaxing scenes. Athletes can develop their own variations, but the most common ones include sitting in a rock-ing chair, lying in a swinging hammock, resting on a beach or sitting in front of an open fireplace. Quite simply, the athlete takes a few moments to close the eyes and view one of these relaxing scenes. The content is fairly irrelevant providing that it has the desired effect. Many athletes have two or more scenes from which to choose when they are looking to calm things down.

Of course, it is also possible for athletes to combine both the breathing and imagery drills. For instance, field event athletes who have 20 minutes or more between jumps or throws might be able to incorporate both of these drills if they need to.

Energizing Techniques

PHYSICAL DRILLS

The third category of techniques is based upon physical activity. If an athlete perceives that he is insufficiently energized then he is advised to 'pump' himself up. Athletes who have become a little lethargic may often be seen performing rapid repetitions of minor muscle group movements in an effort to energize. Good examples include an athlete getting on the ground and doing several press-ups before starting a run-up in the long jump, a rugby player sprinting on the spot while there is a break in play, a sprinter doing some very fast jumping on the spot before a race, or a cricketer chewing his gum very quickly if he has played and missed at a few deliveries.

The athlete has to ensure that the activity chosen for energizing is appropriate. It might need to be performed in a limited space and it should not be an exercise which would fatigue muscles which might contribute to subsequent performance.

IMAGERY DRILLS

The fourth category of short-term self-regulation skills, the Sports Priming Process (SPP), is primarily cognitive in nature. In some respects the form of visualization that is used in cognitive energizing techniques is the same as the SPP described in Chapter Three – but then it is also different. If an athlete feels that he is not 'up enough' before a competition it is possible to change the level of arousal by visualizing or imagining a different scene. For instance, one British middle-distance star would assess his arousal level before races, and if he thought it was too low, he would imagine himself leading the British team out for an Olympic opening ceremony. It was an image that, for him, was guaranteed to raise his heart rate. He would speak frankly about what he could see, and it was obvious that he had given it a lot of thought. He could describe the scene very clearly.

An Australian netballer would replay the image of standing on the Olympic medal podium when she wanted to 'pump herself up'. A British rower replays images of what Portsmouth was like when the ships came home from the Falklands War in 1982. These images are obviously quite different, but they have approximately the same impact on the athletes concerned.

Other strategies include: visualizing a previous race against a top-line athlete, imagining yourself about to compete at a major championships, or imagining yourself in a challenging, but non-sporting situation. Elite athletes have used one or more of these techniques to raise their levels of arousal. Again, these athletes tend to be those who have described themselves as cognitive responders, and typically they have to use energizing techniques on only infrequent occasions. Nevertheless, it is important that the athletes have them at their disposal.

When it comes to working with elite athletes before and during major championships, the combination of somatic relaxation skills and breathing drills is the most effective for reducing arousal levels and controlling tension. They are, if you like, a combination of on-site and off-site self-regulation strategies. The somatic relaxation exercises (described and discussed in the Appendix) can move athletes along the horizontal axis of **Figure 11** quite easily, if the techniques have been well learned. The breathing techniques tend to have a less dramatic effect in terms of horizontal movement, but it has to be remembered that the effect that they do have may be attained in a matter of seconds. The breathing techniques offer a briefer option for self-regulation and they prove to be consistently useful in pressurized sporting environments. By comparison, the 'deeper' techniques may take up to 30 minutes to complete and are invariably completed away from the competition venue.

There is a need for some sophistication in terms of when and where to use each category of the self-regulation techniques. Hence my insistence that athletes take time to learn a variety of them, and that once learned they still practise at least once a week to keep in contact with the skills. In addition, athletes should at first experiment with these techniques before and during training sessions. Then they should build up to use them in minor competitions. Even then there is no substitute for using them in competitive situations.

CHAPTER THREE

The Sports Priming Process

I use imagery before every shot. First I see the ball where I want it to finish, nice and white and sitting up high on the bright green grass. Then I see the ball going there; its path and its trajectory and even its behaviour on landing. The next scene shows me making the type of swing that will turn the previous image into reality.

Jack Nicklaus, world-class golfer

I start thinking about an important match the night before. I visualize what the match will be like and that keeps me from falling asleep. I have a court in my mind and I visualize points. I play the points out inside my head as I think ahead to the next day.

Chris Evert, world-class tennis player

An important aspect of competition preparation is known as visualization or mental rehearsal. I prefer to call my own particular brand of this form of mental training the Sports Priming Process (SPP). Other authors have referred to visualization, sensorization, imagery and mental rehearsal. In general terms they are all talking about the same type of mental conditioning.

Most people daydream. Some more than others, but nearly all allow their minds to go wandering. Children use their imagination almost constantly, but as we grow older we tend to use it less and less. Research from sports institutes and universities around the world is currently suggesting that athletes should be encouraged to daydream and fantasize.

A number of top-class athletes from the 1950s and the 1960s talked about using their imaginations to prepare for events, and this was an early, intuitive form of mental training. People such as the four-times Olympic discus champion Al Oerter talked of picturing himself throwing in a variety of conditions. He would imagine dry throwing circles, wet circles, a left-hander's wind, trailing after five rounds of the competition or competing in a hailstorm. David Hemery, Olympic gold and silver medalist, described his mental preparation for Mexico and Munich, and emphasized his commitment to rehearsing mentally the details of his upcoming event. He would imagine himself running the race from each of the eight lanes on the track. Then, irrespective of which lane he actually drew on the next day, he would be prepared. But while these and many of to-day's athletes were using this technique in an intuitive manner, there is now little doubt that formalized training in mental rehearsal or visualization techniques can enhance performance.

So what is this Sports Priming Process and how can it help athletes? In essence it is a form of skill training that complements the traditional physical practice of skills and movements. Quite simply, the athlete can sit in a comfortable chair or lie on a bed, relax and think about his event or sport. It sounds too good to be true, but we know from much international research that the combination of physical and mental practice is the most effective way of refining a skill. This is particularly true if the athlete is trying to modify an ineffective technique that he has had for years. This situation is almost invariably more difficult than when an athlete is starting from scratch with an entirely new skill. But SPP is not only of use for skill acquisition. It may variously be used for skill maintenance, as well as for pre-event planning and the modification of pre-event arousal states. It is wrong to think of SPP in a narrow sense.

In many respects SPP is nothing more than a sitting down and thinking about sport. Marianne Dickerson, silver medal winner in the World Championships women's marathon, once said, 'My mental preparation for a big race begins weeks before the event. I often find myself mentally picturing myself in the racing situation during workouts. I'll picture myself surging past competitors or crossing the finish line in a certain time. I always try to visualize positive race results.' The successful American distance runner Marty Liquori claimed that, 'if you want to be a champion, you will have to win every race in your mind a hundred times before you win it in real life.'

The idea of mentally practising sports skills has been around for a long time. The research data that were presented in the 1960s and the 1970s showed that improved performances were possible if subjects combined both the physical and the mental aspects of practice. The results were fairly consistent, and I was confident that this approach to skill learning would work with the first group of AIMS athletes.

However, the results achieved with the first two groups were disappointing, and I began to question those reported by others. It was apparent that the subjects described in the journal articles were often undergraduate students who were typically given some form of mental training for four to six weeks. They would go into detailed mental rehearsal when their training session started, and each session would last for about ten minutes. The skills that were practised were novel. In other words, they were new skills that the subjects had previously not experienced.

By comparison, the AIMS 'subjects' were generally older, they were certainly not dealing with a novel task, they were likely to be in training for several years, and each training session would almost certainly last for a longer time. It was not surprising that the successful techniques described in the journals were not 100 per cent appropriate for the AIMS programme. Therefore during the early 1980s I experimented with a number of different ways of approaching this mental training for elite athletes who were entirely familiar with the skills of their chosen events. The Sports Priming Process is the result of the early applied research carried out with elite British track and field athletes and rhythmic gymnasts, as well as with the English netball team.

Why Does SPP Work?

In summary, it helps to 'groove in' the correct blueprint for success and it helps athletes to feel confident that they have been thorough in their preparation. If an athlete becomes effective at the skill of visualization, it is thought that his brain will send stimuli to his muscles in the same sequence as if he were physically doing the same action. The only difference is that their strength will not be large enough to actually make the muscles move. However, when an athlete lies still and mentally rehearses his or her sporting technique it is not uncommon to see various muscles making small, twitching movements.

The academic research is actually of a generally poor standard in this area. There have been many weaknesses in many of the studies. In addition to the 'neuromuscular' theory mentioned above, there are at least two other theories as to why SPP works: symbolic learning theory and bio-informational theory. But as far as AIMS athletes are concerned they do not particularly care about the precise mechanism by which SPP is working for them. They are asked to emphasize seeing and feeling themselves perform with confidence. They believe that this helps them to achieve a level of consistency and, up to a point, it is this belief that matters most.

While some coaches have been teaching versions of visualization for many years, the practice can be optimized by following a few basic ground rules. There are several key features that can enhance such training. These have to be adhered to if this form of training is going to be suuccessful.

Successful implementation of SPP typically requires:

Warming-up

The athlete should use a mental warm-up before the mental rehearsal of the specific event. In other words, if the athlete is attempting to work on a full javelin throw, then he does not start off by imagining lots of throws. Rather, he 'warms-up' his brain before that. This is a significant break with the tradition of classical mental practice techniques.

The warm-up typically involves a brief session with one of the major somatic relaxation skills (see details of these in the Appendix), followed by several minutes of concentration on one or more of the breathing drills. This in turn is followed by visualizing several non-sporting scenes that the athlete is familiar with. These scenes may include virtually anything, but some of the more commonly used are driving a car, walking through a busy shopping centre, watching a television show, washing or showering, packing a suitcase, taking off in an aircraft or climbing sets of stairs.

Experience has shown that the athletes are better able to concentrate on the sporting skill element of the exercise if they have undergone this brief psychological warm-up before the visualization. The warm-up element of the SPP is one feature that has made it a more appropriate technique for the elite athlete.

Athletes have commented that they are virtually conditioned to expect some form of warm-up before every one of their physical training sessions, and that therefore it seems only natural to have one before their mental training sessions.

Imagery

The athlete should re-create a vivid mental picture in which to perform the skills of the event. If the athlete knows that there are certain predominant noises, sights or even smells associated with a specific competition venue, then he should try and imagine those elements of the scene. Some authors have emphasized the need to see everything very clearly in the mental rehearsal, but it is possible to have success with athletes who cannot visualize very well at all. For instance, they may be good at 'feeling' the action from a proprioceptive point of view. Alternatively, one Olympic rowing champion who uses SPP frequently can only 'hear' the rhythm of his event and hence uses the noises within his boat as a cue to his SPP sessions.

The important thing is to try and make the entire scene as realistic as possible in whichever modality the athlete feels comfortable. When an athlete is aroused from the SPP situation I usually ask him questions about the weather conditions, his own form, and how his muscles felt. This encourages him to imagine or experience the scene in as many different modalities as possible.

Timing

The athlete must perform the rehearsal in approximately the correct time frame. I do not find slow-motion replays particularly useful for athletes and in some cases (sprint hurdlers, for example) they have proved to be damaging as far as skill modification is concerned. There is no doubt that incorrect mental practice may be as harmful as incorrect physical practice. The wrong or inappropriate neural blueprints can be established as easily as the correct ones. I have found that elite hurdlers, for example, look for too much detail in their style if they use slow-motion rehearsal, and this thwarts the natural aspect of their hurdling. Therefore I prefer athletes to run races or perform hurdle drills in the true time frame: not too fast and not too slow.

Perfection

The athlete must see himself performing the skills well and positively. The guiding principle has to be 'perfect practice makes perfect'. The emphasis has to be on seeing and feeling things happening correctly. Not only does this help to establish the correct neuromuscular memory, but it also assists in terms of boosting self-confidence. The athlete gets a sense of pleasure and satisfaction from positive mental rehearsal and he knows that he is establishing an efficient skill in the central nervous system.

Steve Backley, a former world record holder in the javelin, has talked and written extensively about how he uses visualization to work on his technique. Interestingly, he sees 'himself' running away from the starting position for his throw. He might have a run-up of 20m or so, and while he is still stationary at the start of his run-up, an 'image' of himself sets off down the runway. Steve actually sees the back of 'himself'. If this image should make some mistake while running away, he will stop the mental rehearsal and wind the 'image' back to himself. He actually uses the analogy of reeling 'himself' in, like a fisherman reeling in a fish on a line. The important thing about this situation is that Steve knows that he does not want to practise errors mentally any more than he wants to rehearse errors physically. His aim is to have perfect SPP sessions.

Looking Within

The athlete should experience the drills or techniques as he would during physical training. In other words, a sprint hurdler sees the hurdles looming up from inside his own eye sockets; he hears the noise of his spikes as he would were he running. When an athlete has learned to use SPP from an internal perspective, he can graduate to external rehearsal. In this mode he would see himself as if someone else were watching him.

The academic literature shows equivocal results in the area of internal versus external visualization. However, from the position of working with elite performers, I have no hesitation in saying that the athlete should start with internal rehearsing before graduating to external rehearsing. In the early 1980s AIMS athletes might have been given an option, but those starting on the internal mode made progress at a faster rate, and hence the advice for more than a decade has been to go from internal to external rather than in the other direction.

Experience has shown that athletes tend to move on to external rehearsal after approximately three months' work on the internal version. Athletes are encouraged to spend two hours per week (probably divided into three or four sessions) using the SPP.

Distorting the Image

For some events at least, athletes deliberately distort some of the details concerning their rehearsal. This typically applies to individual sports where each athlete has a designated lane or area such as running, swimming or shooting. For instance, before running 100m hurdle races, Jane Flemming uses a guided imagery approach which involves her seeing her entire lane being lit up by overhead lights, while the lanes of her opponents are in relative darkness. Darren Clark, the Australian 400m runner, used the image that underneath his lane he could see a brightly-lit neon tube and his opponents did not have this. As he approached the final 150m of his event, it was as if his light got stronger and stronger and 'sucked' him home faster than his opponents. David Jenkins, another world-class 400m runner, used to imagine, before an event, that his race was made up of a series of railway sleepers. Each was positioned to match his stride pattern and he got an extra advantage by being able to hit each of these pieces of wood, while his opponents had to pick their way through them.

It is interesting to note that each of these world-class track athletes was creatively distorting the image to give him or her some sort of advantage against the opponents. It is also interesting to note that while each of these athletes was involved in the AIMS programme, he or she was never advised to create distortions. Independently of each other they chose to develop these slightly off-beat approaches. The same may be said of Steve Backley's fishing-reel approach. I had no input into any of these four variations and yet it is obvious that athletes' imaginations tend to go in this direction naturally.

As athletes become more and more skilled at using SPP, they start to develop small, associated movements while going through the drills. It is not uncommon to see a track athlete's thigh muscles twitch while he is visualizing a race, for example. Another common response is to see the eyes flickering behind the eyelids, almost as if the athlete was seeing a scene unfold. This is known as eye catalepsy and is generally regarded as being a good sign of vivid imagery being experienced.

There are other indications of realistic psychophysiological responses taking place during this form of mental practice. **Figure 15** is a graphic demonstration of what happens to the heart rate when a good visualizer imagines himself running a 400m hurdles race. This example is presented because it relates to one of the best SPP athletes I have had the pleasure of working with. He was a 50-second runner who was inspired by the mental aspects of his event. He was a very keen athlete when it came to dealing with a mental skills programme.

Figure 15 shows that the athlete's heart rate was reduced during the 'warm-up' phase of the SPP, and then increased markedly when he visualized the immediate pre-event environment and the race itself. In the minutes after the race visualization, it may be seen that the heart rate returned to normal. It must be remembered that throughout this activity the athlete was merely lying on the floor. Yet despite this level of physical inactivity he was able to raise his heart rate to over 140 beats per minute. During this type of session he would also breathe quite heavily and perspire profusely. It was as if he had actually run the race. After each session he was able to tell me precisely how he had performed. He could tell me which lane he had competed in, which strip he was wearing, and he could describe the weather conditions.

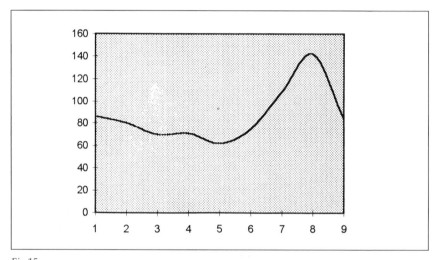

Fig 15

The vertical axis represents heart rate in beats per minute over a 20-minute session. The numbers 1 to 9 represent different stages within the SPP session:

1. Start of athlete consultation session
2. Start of SPP component
3. Somatic relaxation exercises
4. Breathing drills
5. Non-sporting imagery
6. Pre-race imagery
7. Start of race
8. End of race
9. End of session.

When athletes reach this level of sophistication, it is clear that they are utilising SPP to its best advantage. Most athletes can reach this level, but it requires a great deal of practice to become proficient. Like many aspects of this mental skills programme, it requires an investment of time and effort.

SPP skills can be taught to athletes from all sports and they can be encouraged to use the technique regularly throughout their career. In addition, there are certain predictable moments in any athlete's career when he should employ the techniques specifically. Examples are:

- When an athlete is suffering from an injury that prevents him from practising the skills of his event.
- When the athlete has limited access to the required facilities.
- When the athlete is 'out of season' and is primarily concentrating on the conditioning aspect of the programme. It enables the athlete to 'keep his hand in'.
- When an athlete is 'tapering' in the days leading up to a major event and is unlikely to want to do too much physical work.
- In combat sports such as judo or boxing, when the athlete is struggling to find appropriate sparring partners.

The final issue concerning SPP and the AIMS programme relates to the optimal length of time spent visualizing the sporting component of the exercise. For instance, it seems that a 100m runner should be able to visualize for the 10 seconds or so that the race actually takes. But could we expect a marathon runner to visualize for more than two hours? Probably not. To some extent there is a good deal of individual variation. Athletes have different levels of ability in this area.

As a general guideline, athletes can spend up to 15 minutes on the sports component of the SPP session. This could mean multiple repetitions of an event as short as a high jump or a clean and jerk from weightlifting, or a few different scenarios from within a match for a hockey player. A tennis player might rehearse a series of groundstrokes, or a number of different points which make up games. Athletes may choose to replay scenes which have actually occurred in real life, or they may wish to replay the scenes and change some aspect of an event. Or the athletes might 'preplay' events and incidents which have not yet happened. For instance, hockey players might use SPP the night before a game against a known opponent: perhaps imagining themselves against an opponent who marks or who tackles in a certain way. The key component is that the athlete uses SPP and finds himself feeling confident and positive in his own sport.

In 1988 the Australian women's hockey team won the gold medal at the Olympics in Seoul, beating Korea in the final. Before the tournament the likely medalists for the Games were Australia, Korea and the Netherlands (who ultimately won the bronze). Given that the Koreans would be playing in front of their own crowd and that they were a likely medal prospect, it was decided that we should use SPP in the months leading up to the games. The players were taught to visualize various set plays such as penalties and corners, and they were to imagine themselves performing well while inside the Olympic stadium in Seoul.

To supplement the SPP sessions, the players were also asked to play and train with a public address system blearing out loud crowd noises by the side of a pitch. At a training camp held in Canberra we spliced together an audiotape made up entirely from soccer crowd noises. The team played a series of practice matches and had several training sessions under these conditions. The coach was forced to give his half-time team talks with the noise still booming out. Players were forced to practise penalty strokes against this backdrop of noise and distractions.

The entire process was designed to give players and management a sense of preparedness. The athletes would feel that if they were to play against Korea in a medal match, they were as well prepared as possible. In the event, of course, they actually played against Korea for the gold medal. During the match Australia were awarded a penalty stroke and Debbie Bowman, the team captain, was the player to take it. She strode forward confidently and despite the partisan urgings of 27,000 Koreans, she scored with confidence. At the time the score was nil all and the match was very tense.

Australian hockey players and coaches – Olympic champions.

The Australians eventually won 2–0, and in the press conference afterwards Debbie was asked how she felt when she walked up to take the all-important penalty stroke. Despite her obvious euphoric state she replied coolly, 'No, I was very confident. I had done that very same thing hundreds of times before. I knew exactly what I was going to do.' The interviewer did not quite understand and said, 'What? Have you scored hundreds of penalties before?'; Debbie replied, 'No, but I had visualized it hundreds of times before and against an even louder crowd in Canberra!' The interviewer did not really understand what she was talking about, but the team knew very well. They had used rehearsals for a specific situation and those rehearsals had allowed them to feel confident and to play confidently when they were faced with the real life situation. That was and is the aim of the SPP within the AIMS programme.

CHAPTER FOUR

Professional Game Planning

In the last decade many researchers have spent a great deal of time investigating what makes successful athletes different from their less successful counterparts. People such as Orlick and Partington (1988) and Gould, Eklund, and Jackson (1992) studied hundreds of elite performers in an effort to establish the key differences between the 'greats' and the merely 'goods'. Using a variety of in-depth interviews regarding the athletes' best and worst performances, the researchers were able to make a number of generalizations concerning how best to prepare for competition.

One of the most commonly cited findings to appear in the research is that athletes who perform consistently well tend to have a consistent routine or pattern for the way in which they prepare themselves. Pre-performance routines are common in sport at the elite level. The AIMS programme had used this premise long before much of the research was published but it was nevertheless gratifying to see that there was scientific support for what had always seemed common sense. If we want athletes to perform consistently well it seems logical that they should be encouraged to prepare for competition in a similar manner. It is also sensible to allow the athletes the opportunity to experiment with different ways of preparing in order that they may find out what works for them. They should have ownership of the process.

Matthew Pinsent, one of Britain's most successful rowers, has described how he likes to have a pattern for the way in which he prepares for the important races at major championships. At any given rowing World Championships the early part of the week is devoted to the heats, while the latter half focuses on the semi-finals and the all-important final. So while the end of the week is clearly when the medals are handed out, Matthew says, 'I like to get into a routine. I divide the week into a rhythm. On race day I have some "off-time" and some "on-time". I don't like to be focusing hard all day long. I plan to have a gradual build-up during the week. I look for consistency of preparation because I don't want a roller coaster ride! Up and down, up and down.'

The former Olympic sprint champion Valeriy Borzov described his own version of pre-event consistency: 'The first thing to do when it is time to start the warm-up is to estimate the arousal level. However, if the arousal level has been high already a few hours before the start, it is to be hoped that the warm-up jog will reduce it somewhat. Jogging should last until sweating appears. To achieve this within five to seven minutes requires adjustments in running speed. I cover 800 to a 1,000 metres. Following the jog, it is time to work all muscle groups and joints, starting from the neck and finishing with the ankles.'

In the remainder of his interview, Borzov goes on to detail all the elements of his pre-race routine and it is clearly a very thorough approach to preparing for a race. Borzov, and most of the athletes from the eastern European nations, developed and adhered to pre-performance routines. One implied benefit of this approach was that the athlete could influence his level of arousal in a positive manner. The athlete would be in control of the situation.

This process within the AIMS programme is known as Professional Game Planning (PGP). I was first exposed to this concept of consistent preparation by a world-class netball coach named Wilma Shakespear. Herself a former international player, she was the Head Coach at the Australian Institute of Sport during the 1980s. Her experience of touring and playing in England with the Australian team had taught her that there had to be a certain regularity, yet flexibility, in the way that netball teams prepared before a match.

Like most coaches, she would include both physical and mental aspects in a total body warm-up. She would then include individual ball-skill work. Then she moved on to working in pairs before finally ending with small-side games. There was nothing revolutionary about this approach. However, where she was successful was in the way she stuck to this pattern despite many different circumstances being thrown at her teams while touring England. The players had to be able to perform some of this warm-up while on a bus if there were traffic delays in London, for instance. Similarly, they might have to perform some of it in a corridor of a sports centre if they could not gain access to the netball court because a warm-up match was being played on it.

So while she had the ideal warm-up mapped out in her mind (10 minutes of body exercises, followed by 7 minutes of individual hand–eye co-ordination work, followed by 5 minutes of partner work, for instance) , she would also have scaled-down versions of this available to her. This topic would be discussed at length with the players and they had a good understanding about their consistent (within certain limitations) way of preparing for matches. There would be some flexibility to do with outside influences such as traffic delays or cold venues, but for the most part the players knew exactly what to expect when.

Since this approach worked to good effect, it was included in the AIMS programme. The athletes had a high level of control over their own pre-competition preparation, and this fitted in well with the principle of Controlling the Controllables.

In 1986 the Australian Men's Hockey Team, under their coach Richard

Aggiss, introduced elements of the AIMS programme before the World Cup in London. They won the Cup and during the subsequent individual debriefing sessions several of the players stated that the introduction of the concept of PGP had helped to focus attention on the important aspects of the warm-up. This was a team which previously had had a record of falling at the final hurdle and never winning a gold medal. The introduction of a more consistent warm-up may have gone some way to leading to more consistency in performance. Certainly many of the players thought that it made a positive contribution to the team in that competition.

In 1992 the British women's hockey team won the bronze medal in the Barcelona Olympics. Jon Clark was the coach in charge of the two goal-keepers. In conjunction with the keepers, he devised the following PGP for test matches:

Scene: Test Match at 15:00. Team staying at hotel 45 minutes away from venue.

Actions:

10:00.   Two keepers go for a walk together. Discuss relevant features of today's game; for example, known opponents and likely playing conditions. This discussion will allow for better quality visualization later on in the day.

10:30.   Shower or bath. Check kit. Ensure fully prepared by this stage of the morning.

11:00.   One-hour stretch with both keepers. Visualize likely scenarios for this afternoon's match.

12:00–13:45.   Team meeting, lunch, travel to venue.

13:45.   Find warm-up pitch. Light jogging and striding work. Agility exercises.

14:00.   Stretch main goalkeeper-type muscles: groins, thighs, hamstrings. Working as a team of two throughout.

14:15.   Goalkeeping kit on.

14:35.   On pitch for short, sharp warm-up.
Using two outfield substitute players feed mixture of 50 pushes to hands and feet from 6m away.
Two feeding players: mixture of 50 hits and undercuts at $3/4$ pace from 10m.
Repeat for keepers on knees.
Three to 5 feeders spread around top of circle. Mixture of pushes, hits and undercuts. Feeders allowed to pick up rebounds.

14:50.   Drinks, final team talk, stick check and final technical reminders.

This PGP was used from August 1991 onwards. It was modified in one or two ways, but essentially remained the same for twelve months leading

Former world record holding javelin thrower Steve Backley is highly adept at pre-event strategy.

up to the games. Before this approach neither of the two goalkeepers had prepared in precisely this manner, but over time they adjusted their own individual approaches until this consistent style suited their personalities. They had a large say in the precise nature of the routine.

PGP may also be used to good effect by individual athletes. Again, there has to be an element of flexibility in the execution (organizers have been known to make last minute adjustments to schedules) but the ground rules are the same. A real life example of a former world-record holder in race walking is included here by way of explanation. This letter to the athlete came as a result of two or three meetings to discuss this particular approach. It is a summary of those meetings and is reproduced here in essentially its original form.

Dear David,

I have given some thought to your pre-race segmenting , and I've added a bit more detail here and there. If you decide to compete next weekend I'd like you to use this schedule or at least one that is very much like it. In other words, it's important that there's quite a full content.

It would be good if you could use it, just to practise the Professional Game Planning. I appreciate that you are recovering from injury, but perhaps this is all the more reason why you should experiment with it this weekend when there will be little pressure on you to break another world record!

4 hours pre-race: meal.

3–2.5 hours: toilet and reaffirmation of the race objectives. In this current context this would probably mean to walk conservatively and get used to that type of pace.

2 hours: organize uniform and bag. Have a shower and while in the shower visualize the last two minutes before the gun. Get dressed and relax.

1.5 hours: read and relax. The last thing you do before leaving for the warm-up area is to write your key word on the back of your hand. For this first attempt might I suggest from that list of concentration words narrow, as in narrow focus on the key objective?

1 hour: travel to warm-up area.

45 minutes: long, slow work/drills/mobility.

30 minutes: stretching. During this next 5-minute period it's important that you focus in on your key word and have a conversation with yourself to reaffirm the reason for your precise preparation.

25 minutes: final toilet/check shoes and apply Vaseline. After the Vaseline once again look at your hand and remind yourself of your major goal.

20 minutes: do some strides, but don't do any faster than race pace stuff. I think it's better to stay in control here rather than getting the heart-rate up too much.

15 minutes: monitor body and mental check. Clench and unclench the fist quite close to the face so as to emphasize the key word.

10 minutes: do some more passive stretching, and during part of this close your eyes and visualize how the first 400m will pan out. Make sure it's a vivid reconstruction including weather conditions, sounds and sights. Visualize positive start – that is, a conservative one.

5 minutes: control nerves and reaffirm the purpose of this race. Aim to have a degree of 'butterflies', but be in control of them.

1 minute: stare at the back of the hand relentlessly and in the last few seconds be silently repeating the word to yourself. This should almost be like the chanting of a mantra by Buddhist monks.

Finally , you then execute the policy as planned. If you start to doubt it or yourself, then you must quote the key word over and over again.

By the time I next see you, you should be able to recite this plan or your version of it to me. Learn it, rehearse it and then do it! Good luck!

This athlete went on to make two or three significant changes to the precise contents of this PGP, but this was perfectly acceptable. The athlete had control of this programme and he fully accepted ownership of it. Ultimately, this is one of the goals of the AIMS programme. PGP is not one of the more complicated skills utilized within elite sport. In fact, it might be argued that it is one of the simplest. Therefore there can be no logical explanation or excuse as to why athletes do not use it more regularly. Coaches ask for more consistency from performers, and this would appear to be an easy approach to learning it. All athletes are encouraged to experiment with this form of training.

However, it has to be noted that the use of PGP is not, by itself, going to ensure a high level of performance. There may be a 'flip' side to the practice. The Irish swimming star Michelle Smith won three gold medals in the Atlanta Olympics as well as a bronze. She has described her own form of PGP very eloquently:

There is a call-up room outside the Olympic pool where they check off your name; you have to be there 15 minutes before your event. But in Atlanta it was a little more relaxed; so I would check my name in, go back to the tunnel area and then come in at the very last minute. There is a lot of psyching out in the call-room. I would wait until the last minute to go into the call-room, then walk in and let all the other girls watch me without looking at anyone. While they were working out what sort of form I was in, I would start swinging, stretching and preparing. Most of them would sit down, but I would remain standing.

She also commented that she would eat the same food at the same time before the event, and that she would arrive at the venue exactly 45 minutes before her race. But having won gold medals in her three events at Atlanta, she was then favourite for the gold in her fourth, the 200-m butterfly. In the call-room before the event her goggles broke. Her routine was thrown out and she panicked when she could not find her coach/husband who had a spare pair. She ended up rushing around beneath the stadium looking for him and, when she could not find him, she finally borrowed an oversize pair from a Dutch swimmer. During this time she had not been able to use her 'psych-out' technique in the call-room and by the time she did return to the room the other swimmers were already being marched out on to the pool deck.

She commented, 'My concentration was gone. I was standing on the blocks worrying about my goggles. I tried to put it to the back of my mind. I tried to forget about it, but it threw me off my guard.' Although Michelle did not use it as an excuse, she somewhat underperformed in that race and won 'only' a bronze medal. This incident highlights the dangers on relying on too rigid a PGP. Michelle's normal mode of preparation was thrown out and she suddenly found herself thinking about inappropriate things immediately before an Olympic final.

CHAPTER FIVE

Focusing in Sport

When I began rowing, someone told me that in every stroke there are 168 things that can go wrong. Now I disagree; there are more. I have a mental checklist with hundreds of things on it – watch hand levels, power with the legs, good body posture, and so on. I try to get through this list with as many 'yeses' as possible. You have to have a dedication to the thought process.

Marnie Mcbean, four-time Olympic gold medalist in rowing and sculling

You can't be thinking 200m ahead or you won't be able to do what you're supposed to. When the race starts, I take it one stroke at a time.

Wendy Wiebe, world champion lightweight sculler

I have learned to cut out all of the unnecessary thoughts – the circular fears and hesitations that get in the way. I simply concentrate. I concentrate on the tangible – on the track, on the race, on the blocks, on the things I have to do. The crowd fades away and the other athletes disappear and now it's just me and this one lane.

Michael Johnson, three-time Olympic gold medalist in sprints

Chapter One included an explanation of Hierarchical Goal Setting in which there are three types of goal: outcome, performance and process. It was suggested that the most important component was process and several examples were presented to show that athletes should focus their goal setting on the mechanisms of success rather than just the result they wanted to achieve.

AIMS athletes are encouraged to take this approach to goal setting for two reasons: first, this is an efficient way of attaining goals during the build-up to a competition season and, secondly, because this is the very type of focus that will be required during the event itself. Athletes clearly want to win, but to improve their chances of winning they should be focusing on the processes or mechanisms which will enable them to do so.

Silken Laumann, the medal-winning Canadian sculler commented that in her key races she focuses on process goals, 'I obviously want to win if I can. I focus on myself and rowing my own race. I do not know where the other boats are. I have to keep pressure on myself because there is no cox to do that for me. I keep giving myself pressure calls to attack. I focus on my legs and I stay aggressive. I do not think about the result.'

Similarly, the Canadian Olympic sprint gold medalist Donovan Bailey comments on his focus during races. In his press conference after winning the gold and breaking the world record in Atlanta in 1996 he said, 'I was not thinking about the world record. When I go into a race thinking about times I always screw it up, so I was thinking about my start and trying to relax. Just focus on doing the job at hand.'

In 1996 it was also interesting to hear the comments from Ric Charlesworth the coach to the Australian women's hockey team before their gold medal match with Korea. Rather than talking about 'Win, win, win', he was focusing much more on the process goals. He said, 'We will have to control the tempo of the game. We must get the ball and keep it. We must have close marking and good positioning. We will have to be disciplined. We have to use our variations on the corners. We are happy with this process.'

Australia also won the gold medal in 1988, and the then coach Brian Glencross also focused on process goals with the team. Naturally they wanted to win every hockey match they played, but he worked hard so that the players would not be distracted and devised specific strategies for specific phases of each match. For instance, the statistics from top-class hockey matches show that after a goal is scored there is a strong possibility that another goal will be scored within a minute or two. This goal is often scored by the opposition. Brian and his assistant coach, Peter Freitag, reasoned that this probably occurs, in part, because the scoring team relax somewhat or play in a more 'cavalier' style.

Accordingly for Seoul in 1988, the team developed a Goal Action Plan (GAP) to be employed as soon as they had scored a goal. This was simply that for the next five minutes they would play in a more conservative style and would mark the opposition tightly. They would hang on to the ball and not take too many risky options. The GAP system was worked on in 1987 and 1988, and when a goal was scored, all the players could be heard calling out, 'GAP, GAP!'. They reminded each other about the appropriate focus for those few minutes.

Similarly the 1988 Australian team worked out a strategy for focusing when the opposition were 'on a roll'. It is a feature of hockey, and to a lesser extent of soccer, that even when one team is clearly better than the other, the weaker team will still have some passages of play when things are going their way. They might effectively 'camp' in the opposition's final quarter of the pitch. This is totally normal and predictable. The trick is to ride out this storm and then gradually apply pressure to the opposition. The situation is often referred to as one team having the 'psychological momentum', and this may also be seen by individuals in sports such as tennis and squash.

Within the Australian hockey team a few key players were identified who could make the call known as 'Danger!'. Despite the particular word chosen, this was not a panic call. It simply meant that when it was made, all players were to recognize that the opposition were 'on a roll' and that each team member should avoid high-risk, 'fancy' play for the next few minutes. It was similar to the GAP call, although there were various tactical differences. In essence it was asking players not to try heroic, high-risk skills which might not come off and which would lead to more pressure being applied to the Australian defence.

Although the precise calls were different, similar processes were adopted by the medal-winning British women's hockey team in Barcelona in 1992. In both teams the coaches were simply trying to get the players to focus on appropriate processes during certain predictable phases of a match. Feedback from the players suggested that this approach helped during some of the harder Olympic matches.

The Canberra Raiders Rugby League team are a world-class force in the game. In 1988 they used parts of the AIMS programme under their coach Tim Sheens. This was a very successful team, and included some experienced and gifted players such as Mal Meninga, Peter Jackson, Ricky Stuart and Laurie Daley. They developed an equivalent process to the hockey players' 'Danger'. They were concerned with defending their 'Red Zone' – their own 22-metre area. They wanted to stop the opposition scoring and wanted to heighten their concentration within this area of the pitch. The call was 'Red Zone' and it referred to low-risk tactics and a grim determination in all tackles. Tim Sheens built on the approach of the women's hockey team in developing his own team-specific processes.

Attentional Styles

Another element of focusing within the AIMS programme is based around the intuitive work of Bob Nideffer from America. Bob is an interesting and experienced individual. He is married to a world-ranked

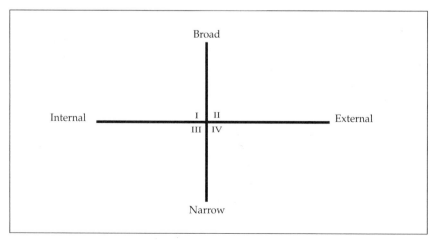

Fig 16

Jane Flemming (no. 4) prior to the start of a hurdles race.

tennis player, was a top-class diver himself and an Aikido black belt, he writes extensively and was an American team sport psychologist in Seoul in 1988.

Nideffer has made many contributions to the world of sport psychology, but perhaps he is most famous for his work on attentional styles. His work is not without controversy, and he has been criticized for taking too simple a view of the matter. Nevertheless, his theory does have an intuitive appeal, and athletes certainly seem to agree with many of his ideas.

Nideffer (1976) suggests that the focus of concentration moves along two intersecting dimensions in response to the changing demands of different situations. At any given point in time, an individual's focus of concentration may be described on the basis of its width (is it broad or narrow?), and its direction (is it external or internal?). **Figure 16** shows four different types of concentration used by human beings every day.

It is clear that different situations require different concentration strategies. This is a basic premise on which the AIMS programme is based. Nideffer suggests that there are in summary four different attentional or concentration styles available to us:

1. A broad-internal focus of concentration is the style used for reviewing the 'big picture'. This could be a coach making selection decisions about players or substitutions, for instance.

2. A broad-external focus of concentration is used to interpret and react quickly to the environment. Team sport players in particular might spend a fair amount of time using this attentional style as they choose where to run to or whom to pass to.

3. A narrow-internal focus is used to organize and rehearse systematically an activity such as a gymnastic routine.

4. A narrow-external focus of concentration is the type of attention required to execute a narrow-defined skill such as kicking a ball, sinking a putt or taking a shot in soccer or hockey.

The difference between a narrowly-internal focus and a broad-internal focus is that in the narrow form an individual is attending to immediate issues or problem solving in the present. A broad-internal focus often involves the recalling of past information and blending that with the present to predict the future.

Interestingly, focusing exclusively in an external direction or an internal one, may be either extremely positive or extremely negative. When the performance situation is one that requires an exclusively external or internal focus and the athlete has the skills and abilities to meet the requirements of it, he may enter the 'zone' no matter what the direction of focus is. However, when the performance situation requires a different type of concentration from the one currently engaged in and the athlete is unable to shift, major problems may occur, including extreme panic and 'choking'.

Some research has demonstrated that increasing emotional arousal causes an involuntary narrowing of the focus of attention. In other words, the athlete focuses on the object which is causing the arousal in the first place. Other research has also suggested that increasing levels of anxiety can lead to a reduction in attentional flexibility. It may be that emotional arousal not only influences an athlete's ability to shift concentration voluntarily along the broad to narrow dimension; it could also affect his ability to shift from an internal to an external focus.

Certainly this theory seemed to fit quite well with the elite team-sport players who have been involved with the AIMS programme. Any players will find that they are constantly changing their focus of attention during a match, and they probably make thousands of changes in every game. For one second, the player about to take the free hit is using a broad focus of attention. He or she is taking in cues from all over the pitch. Who is in free space? Who is tightly marked? Where is the umpire? But they might also be using an internal mode as well as they remember what the coach had said about tactics in this half of the pitch, or what they know about the opposing goal keeper's weak spots.

Eventually the player chooses an option, and then rapidly switches to a narrow focus as he or she hits the ball. Based upon that act the switch is then made back to a decision-making mode (internal style) and the decision on what to do next. An elite player who possesses various 'automatic' skills will make such switches constantly throughout a match and will probably be unaware that this computation is going on at all. It seems natural because this happens in most training sessions and every match.

However, the problem comes when and if the anxiety becomes so great (or perhaps even the physical fatigue is too great) that the players lose attentional flexibility. For instance, the player about to take a free hit appreciates that there are only two minutes to go and the need to score a goal to force the match into extra time. He or she is too anxious and gets locked in the broad focus of attention. This player is still capable of reading the situation and making a good tactical decision, but is unable to focus narrowly enough and makes a hash of it at the point of actually hitting the ball.

Or that same player, still faced with all the anxiety, is locked in a narrow attentional style. He managed to hit the ball well but, because he could not really focus on any broader issues, failed to see that the player he was passing to was in an offside position. In either situation where the player has lost attentional flexibility the result is the same – a wasted free hit and probably an angry coach and a disappointed player. Imagine what happens to the resultant level of anxiety and imagine what would happen if the same scenario, a free hit, presented itself a minute later.

Of course, it may not be that Nideffer's theory on attentional style and attentional narrowing is entirely correct. For instance, Michael Eysenck (1992) has talked about such factors as anxiety leading to individuals having less effective working capacity available to them because they waste resources on worry or other task-irrelevant issues, or becoming hyperdistractable when under pressure.

Applied practice is not necessarily dictated by waiting to see which one, if either, is ever proved correct in this area. Suffice it to say that elite team-sport players can certainly recognize some of the symptoms associated with the unfortunate player described above. They are less concerned with the precise mechanisms occurring inside their heads – they are more interested in solutions.

The solutions within the AIMS programme naturally centred on the themes of process goals, variations on 'GAP' and 'Danger', anxiety reductions techniques (see Chapter Two), re-focus exercises and the use of positive self-talk.

In the specific hockey example, the solution might be to have the player spend the next few moments in the match concentrating on something very small and virtually impossible to achieve. Typically the player would know to try and focus on the small dimples or the brand logo on the hockey ball, or that on the hockey sticks. This activity can act as a brief distracter and has been known to help players break out of the attentional inflexibility problem.

As a sport, golf presents some interesting problems with regards to attentional style, and perhaps more interestingly, attentional capacity. A round of tournament golf may take approximately four hours. Yet for the professionals taking only seventy shots or so, the active part of the round adds up to only about two minutes of work. Much of the remainder of the time is spent walking from shot to shot. The AIMS programme suggests that it is unreasonable to ask a player to concentrate narrowly and with intensity for four hours. Instead it seems more appropriate to ask for a certain intensity of concentration for that vital two minutes. Accordingly, a golfer should be switched into a narrowness once the club selection and shot selection have been made. He then plays his shot, spends a few moments learning from it, and walks off in the direction of the ball. During this walk the mind can be allowed to take in a variety of stimuli, perhaps even involving conversation and certainly allowing the brain to 'tune out' from the golf shot for a few moments.

However, if the player has a 200-metre walk to his next shot, he needs to 'zoom in' at a certain point. A golfer can be encouraged to draw an imaginary circle around the ball. When the player reaches this line (perhaps some 20m from the ball) and steps into the circle then the shot-specific concentration style returns, complete with such elements as judging distance, wind conditions and club selection. In the 200m walk he was probably not focusing narrowly, but he certainly has to now.

Typically the golfer then goes through his pre-shot rituals, plays the shot, assesses it and again sets off in pursuit of the ball. This pattern should remain fairly constant throughout the round. The exception might be around the putting green where there is relatively little time between shots.

Re-Focusing in Sport

Much of the work on re-focusing has been conducted by athletes and coaches. There is little written about it in the research literature. Re-focus techniques typically use some relatively minor physical movements to allow the brain a few seconds to start to focus on appropriate stimuli. Athletes will talk about 'getting their brains in gear' and this is where re-focusing comes into play.

Examples are highly sport-specific, but it is as if the minor physical movement is accompanied by some unspoken paragraph or sentence from a coach. For instance, AIMS netballers who miss a simple shot for goal might be seen to do two quick squeezes of their playing bib or top. The squeezes are like a memory aid to remind them to forget about that mistake, get back into the present tense, and focus on offering a good position for their team-mates to pass to. Or an AIMS squash player who makes an unforced error and loses a point might be seen to be squeezing his racquet handle. The player is literally trying to squeeze out the mistake, and one elite performer even talked about seeing a 'puddle' of the mistake appearing on the floor. An AIMS rugby player who misses a tackle, might be seen to make a fist and throw it away. This is almost as if the mistake is being thrown into a rubbish bin.

There are many other sport-specific variations, but each one comes complete with the sentence which says, 'OK that has happened, it's history, so let's now prepare for my next involvement.' By itself, any minor physical movement is not going to make an athlete a better performer. But the movement and the few words said silently combine to make an excellent re-focusing tool. Athletes and coaches from rowing, rugby, soccer, netball, basketball, squash, tennis, hockey and the throwing events in track and field have all used re-focusing with a certain degree of success.

Re-focusing does not always relate to competing – it also has a role in the training activities within some sports. Silken Laumann, the successful oarswoman, once said, 'I find that my mind tends to wander on long workouts. After 90 minutes of straight rowing I sometimes realise I've lost my focus and have begun thinking about making a 'phone call I need to make or something. When this happens I devise what could be called concentration games. By forcing myself to think only about how I'm using my legs over the next 500m, for example, I'm able to block out the distracting thoughts.'

Self-Talk

Chapter Nine includes a section specifically dealing with self-talk and the injury rehabilitation process; but self-talk is also of great importance to an athlete during an event itself. Self-talk is a term coined to describe the inner dialogue that athletes have. What athletes say to themselves is critical to performance. The trick is to gain control of this 'conversation' and this is not always easy. The thoughts affect both feelings and actions and they are therefore important to the athlete's performance. Inappropriate thoughts can often lead to poor decisions and performances. Of course, strategies such as focusing on processes such as GAP are forms of self-talk. It is hoped that the hockey players interpreted GAP along the following lines, and the Australian goalkeeper Kathy Partridge, when asked what GAP meant said:

> OK GAP has been called. That's good – it means we are going to be playing with the same theme in mind. We've prepared for this and we all know our jobs. We've done this loads of times before. This will soon snuff out their hopes of getting an equaliser. This will break their hearts!

Athletes who achieve at the highest level in sport seem to evolve their own intuitive versions of self-talk. Perhaps having experienced the difference between success and failure they learn which 'words' work for them. If they use certain statements they tend to get their mind back on track during a match or competition. When they do not use these statements they tend to get disappointing results and hence they work out for themselves what is and is not appropriate.

However, less experienced athletes may not find this an easy step to take, so much of the AIMS programme in this area is designed to guide them through the process. The textbooks would describe the technique as cognitive restructuring, but the AIMS athletes would simply refer to it as 'thought control'. Over a series of several meetings an athlete is likely to be able to describe several performances where the results were not very good. With the right coaxing it might be possible to find out what the athlete thought about during them, and even what they said to themselves during the stages of that competition.

If patterns emerge, and there are some negative words or statements that are common, then it is possible to 'match' these with other, more positive variations. For instance, the rower who might have performed below par in the past and who while doing so kept repeating the sentence, 'I must not shorten up the stroke too much when I get tired', could be encouraged to replace it with a positive alternative. This might be, for example, 'I will keep my stroke long throughout the race', or 'I've done the extra fitness work, so I'll stay long all race!'

The theory behind thought control is simple. Find out if there are any negatives which are used on a regular basis. If there are, then replace them with something positive. If the theory is simple then the execution can be quite complex. It can take several sessions, sometimes informal ones, before much progress is made. I am keen to capitalize on 'teachable moments' when working with athletes and teams. These are informal opportunities such as finding yourself in a dinner queue with an athlete, or sitting next to one on a bus or aircraft. The process of breaking down some of the old 'negatives' can involve almost constant reinforcement and hence I am happy to utilize these 'teachable moments' when they arise.

Athletes on the AIMS programme are also encouraged to discuss the common categories of negative self-talk. In the early days of the AIMS programme this topic was avoided. It was considered that if the athletes were not using too much negative self-talk, then why bother to tell them about all of the other types that have been used in the past? But over time it seemed that most of the athletes came into contact with them anyway, so perhaps it was better to discuss them in advance. The approach is to say something like, 'Hey, you'll never guess what some athletes are daft enough to say to themselves ?' This is then described by examining six or seven categories. This list was discussed with the British rowing team during the build-up to Atlanta in 1996 and is reproduced essentially in its original form.

Catastrophizing

Major league over-exaggerating, for instance, you get a knee injury and you say to yourself 'I'll never be able to compete again!'

Overgeneralization

Incorrectly extending the expected impact of something to aspects of something not likely to be affected, for instance, following a wrist injury, you say, 'I'll probably lose my leg strength as well.'

Selective Abstraction

Attending to specific aspects of a situation that have little impact on the 'bigger picture': 'The last athlete with this injury didn't recover, and neither will I.'

Absolutistic Thinking

Simplistically reducing complex experiences to all-or-nothing categories: 'My warm-up wasn't very good so my race will be lousy!'

Crystal-ball Gazing

Guessing about the future, for instance, 'If we don't beat at least three crews in this race, the coaches will probably drop one or more of us.'

Mind Reading

Guessing how other people are thinking: 'Based upon how I'm rowing today the coach must think I'm an idiot.'

The rowers were then encouraged to discuss ways of avoiding these types of thinking. They decided to be their own policemen and monitor any such 'violations'. Interestingly, they also thought that athletes who were likely to verbalize variations of this (so no longer merely self-talk) were more likely to be using this as self-talk as well. So they set up a bigger 'policing' exercise in which they monitored what each other actually said. This was all done in a light-hearted manner, but nevertheless it did reinforce the implied importance to this area.

Slump Busting in Team Sports

The Americans are prone to talk about players being in a slump when they have had a few matches where the performance was somewhat below par. Much time and effort is spent on 'slump busting' as teams try to get athletes to return to form. While the term slump busting is not a formal part of the AIMS programme, it has to be acknowledged that many coaches of team sports tend to be interested in this topic. The AIMS programme has been utilized by many team players in the last fifteen years. The list has included medal- winning hockey players, professional soccer players in England, professional rugby league players in Australia, a few New Zealand All-Blacks, international cricketers and world champion netballers.

From this sample of elite performers it is clear that most players do have a relative slump at some point during their career, and this is perhaps inevitable when one considers the large number of matches often played by these athletes. When an athlete or coach asks for advice in this area, he is normally directed to look at what is it that the player is focusing on during his matches. After a few minutes of any such discussion it normally appears that the player is concentrating on trying to break out of the slump and keeps experimenting with many different technical features of his game.

The advice from the AIMS programme is to forget this approach and instead imagine that there is some great sporting guru sitting up in the stand, watching and evaluating the player's contribution to the match. Quite simply, this guru has two columns on the evaluation sheet. One says 'Positive' and the other 'Negative'. At the end of the match, the guru will simply want to compare the number of positives with the number of negatives. The key to this approach is that the player gets one positive tick if the pass was an accurate 3-metre one to his colleague standing almost next to him, and he still gets only one tick if it had been a brilliant

50-metre pass which found an unmarked colleague much further upfield.

The principle about this approach is to rebuild self-confidence and the best way to do that is to simplify the task so that there is a greater chance of success. The player should be focusing on doing many low-risk moves which are likely to make an overall positive contribution to the team. He will be playing himself out of the slump and should simply be thinking about the ways in which he can add to his tally of positives.

Obviously if the player is the star of the team and it is the final, medal-winning game of the season and the coach needs a virtuoso performance from him, then the 'great guru in the sky' routine may not be popular with the coach. However, if that is the situation then something radical certainly has to be tried anyway.

Winning Words

When working with elite performers, it is often a good idea to find some 'simple' ideas for the athletes to use as an anchor. This is not as insulting as it may sound. When athletes are performing in highly pressured environments they often prefer simplicity with regards to any coaching input. Athletes will often use the cliché, 'less is more' when describing how much input they want from their mentors. Accordingly, many coaches have asked for advice with regard to what to say, and, perhaps more importantly, what not to say to athletes before events. I have listed some of the sayings or clichés that have been used effectively at the Olympic level. Each is accompanied by a brief explanation, but clearly either the coach or myself would have added some individual elements to each remark.

Person in the Mirror

When appealing to an athlete's sense of personal challenge we often use the image that the enemy is actually the person he sees in the mirror when he gets up in the morning. In other words, the athletes are in control of their own thoughts and attitudes, and they must not let the person in the mirror defeat them. That person is the first one they need to overcome to have a great performance. That person is also the one they will live with for the rest of their lives and therefore it seems totally illogical to allow that person to plant negative or self-defeating thoughts.

Giving the Opposition Permission to Dominate You

These words are particularly pertinent to team-game players when faced with an opposition who are very good. Typically 'we' are the underdogs in this situation. Team sports often produce a number of 'match-ups' in which our goal defence in netball, for instance, will be matched against a known goal attack from the opposition. If the known opponent is something of a star it could be that our player is faced with a long and painful encounter in the ensuing match.

We then take the approach that the opponent can only dominate our player if he gives the opponent his permission to do so. This is quite a frightening prospect for any self-respecting athlete. It is as if we are saying that , yes, their particular player may be 'better' than ours, but he refuses to be dominated by that player. The player must keep fighting and struggling to make life difficult for this opposition star player. If he does not, then he is confessing that he allowed himself to be walked over by the opposition.

This saying has been used effectively with Olympic teams during half-time breaks. This is especially true if one or two key players seem to be performing below par. These words have been delivered to the team, but the eye contact made it perfectly clear which players could do a little more. In most instances those players have gone on to increase their efforts significantly.

Anger Is Ambition Without the Ammunition

Some athletes, especially males, think that if they get themselves angry at the opposition, they are likely to play or compete well. While this strategy may work effectively, it typically will only work on one or two occasions. To calm some of our hotheads, the idea that having the ambition without the ammunition is quite a vivid one: they would hate to find themselves in a fight without any ammunition!

Leave the Pitch with a Headache

To emphasize the need to keep focusing on the correct cues during a sporting encounter, we use the prompt that athletes should leave the pitch or the pool with a headache. In most team sports, for example, it is accepted that performers will be physically drained when they leave the playing area, but we also stress that they should be mentally drained – hence the headache idea. Success in team sports does not rely totally on going out and playing like the Kamikaze for the first 15 minutes only to find yourself with no energy reserves as the match progresses. It is a combination of physical and mental application that leads to success.

Make Each Day Your Masterpiece

These words have been used most effectively when athletes have been at major events and there is some time before the competition begins. Obviously its roots are in the concept of living in the present. The athletes are told that they wake up and have a blank canvas to work with. They will decide what this canvas will be filled with – both the quantity and the quality. The theme is aimed at getting them to accept responsibility for their actions both at and away from the sports venue.

Any Performance Is Making a Statement about Yourself

This comment is designed to get a certain consistency of application across all training sessions and all competitions. For elite performers, it can be difficult to maintain a high-quality focus if a competition is not particularly important. They may not need to be at their very best if the opposition is a little weak. However, it is dangerous for them to develop the habit of playing or training at a level slightly below their best. A useful way of avoiding this is to appeal to their own egos with the observation that at any time they train or compete they are making a statement about themselves and surely they would not want to make one to the effect that they are casual or shoddy?

I Am R.E.A.D. but not Quite Ready

This strange observation was used by Derek Redmond, the former member of Britain's world champion 4x400-metre relay team. His career was dogged by injuries but he nevertheless competed with distinction. In the Barcelona Games of 1992 he tore his hamstring in the semi-final and his father famously emerged from the crowd to help his son limp across the line. Before this sad event, Derek was getting faster and faster in every training session.

He was using elements of the AIMS programme and during one of our sessions at the games, I casually asked him how were things going. His reply was full of confidence. He said that he was R.E.A.D. and although he was not completely READY, he was only missing the letter Y. This would come in the next day or two. The point about Derek's saying, which I have subsequently used on several occasions, is that there is little point in being completely ready until the maximum performance is required. The experienced athlete paces himself to be able to give the optimum performance on the crucial day.

The Bumble Bee Doesn't Know It Can't Fly

Aerodynamically, the bumble bee cannot fly – its body is too heavy and its wings are too weak. Thankfully, the bee cannot understand English, does not know what the experts are saying about it, and so carries on flying anyway! The message is clear to the athletes. Do not limit your expectations on the basis of comments from other people. Sport has many examples of athletes who have been told that they are too small, too old, or too slow, and yet they have gone on to be world beaters.

Derek Redmond – he's R.E.A.D. but not quite ready.

If not You, then Who? If not Now, then When?

I first heard about this saying in 1991 when the legendary pole vaulter Sergei Bubka credited his sport psychologist with planting these words in his mind. They had a good impact on him and they have been used within the AIMS programme to good effect. When Garry Herbert coxed the Searle brothers to their gold-medal rowing performance in the 1992 Games, he was screaming these words at the brothers as they raced towards the finishing line. The message was received and understood.

Inanimate Objects Have No Brains

When talking to a rower it is often worth reminding him that the oar does not have a brain. The same can be said of a hockey player and his stick or a javelin thrower and his javelin. The statement is an obvious one, but it helps to remind the athlete that the implement will simply do what it is told to do. It has no brain and no say in the matter. In certain tense situations it may sometimes be as if the object has taken on a life of its own, but this is clearly nonsense.

Pressure Hurts but Sustained Pressure Kills

This saying is in some way related to the earlier topic of teams being 'on a roll' for certain passages within a game. In this instance, these words are used when a team is likely to be in the ascendancy. Perhaps when we are the prematch favourites, but we are concerned not to become complacent. Some good teams get the upper hand in sporting contests, but then start coasting. As a consequence, the opposition start to get a sense that all is not lost. They raise their game and suddenly the result is in danger. The emphasis on sustained pressure is the key and most coaches have been keen to use this terminology and this saying. Once a team gets ahead it must go on to finish the job and these words have been used to ensure this focus.

Sho Fujimoto Wins Gold Medal with Broken Leg

Japanese gymnast Sho Fujimoto is a legendary Olympic figure. As a member of the Japanese team in Montreal in 1976 he won a gold medal in the team competition, despite the fact that he had broken his leg and still had two pieces of apparatus to complete. If he failed to complete the event, then the USSR would win the gold. Historic footage shows him landing on his broken leg as he came off one apparatus and yet he stood still and was awarded enough points for Japan to win.

The story itself is moving enough, but when coupled with the things he said afterwards (for instance, he commented that he felt he had to do it for his team mates who had trained so hard) it can be very powerful. A relatively small man, with a huge heart was prepared to go through enormous pain in search of glory. This story has been used effectively with many athletes who are a little below par or who are carrying an injury before an event.

Don Schollander's Water with the Pinkish Tinge

The quotation below has been used effectively with athletes before a mjor event. I am loath to call it a pre-competition 'psych-up', but it has had some important results with elite performers. The theme is one of trying just that little bit harder, and *enjoying* the suffering that goes with the experience. Don Schollander won five Olympic gold medals in swimming and he certainly knew how to push himself to the limits.

> As you approach the limit of your endurance, it begins coming on gradually, hitting your stomach first. Then your arms grow heavy and your legs tighten – thighs first, then the knees. You sink lower in the water as if someone was pushing down on your back. You experience perception changes. The sounds of the pool blend together and become a crashing roar in your ears. The water takes on a pinkish tinge. Your stomach feels as though it's going to fall out – every kick hurts like heck – and suddenly you hear a shrill, internal scream... It is right here, at the pain barrier, that the great competitors are separated from the rest.

Working Harder

I normally use two quotations from the world of boxing. Muhammad Ali was arguably the greatest ever fighter and Jeff Fenech was an Australian who won many world titles. The two comments are different, but they send the same message to aspiring champions – do the little extra it takes to become champion.

Ali comments,

> Before I get in the ring, I'd have already won or lost it out on the road. The real part is won or lost somewhere far away from witnesses – behind the lines, in the gym and out there on the road long before I dance under those lights.

Fenech adds,

> A true champion can push himself to the limit and then go further. A lot of people want to achieve things but never do. A champion gets in there and does whatever is necessary to meet his goal. He will fight one more round, run that extra kilometre, make that last-ditch tackle. The great ones have minds that demand the supreme effort and bodies that can respond.

Associative and Dissociative Thoughts in Endurance Sports

Another component within the AIMS programme which examines focusing in sport deals with associative and dissociative thoughts in endurance sports. An associative style of thinking might relate to the direction of attention being focused on feedback from the body. In other words, the athlete is listening to his body and using the cues he gets for things such as pace judgement. For instance, he might 'listen' to feedback from his calf muscles while running a marathon race. He knows that he has to look after his body to be able to endure the significant discomfort associated with the event. Dissociative thoughts, by comparison, mean virtually the opposite. In this style of thinking the athlete would rather think about anything else other than the feedback from his body.

There has been some contradictory research published in this area. For instance, at one time it was proposed that elite performers should use associative and the non-elite use predominantly dissociative strategies. Then researchers looked at the variables of experience, sport and training or competing. But much of the research has been inconsistent.

However, the AIMS programme is unequivocal with regards to events such as race walking, distance events in swimming and marathon running. In relative terms, these events are not complex motor skills. Clearly, they do require skill, but perhaps they do not contain the same intricacies as gymnastics or ball sports. In 1988 Lisa Martin won the silver medal in the Olympic marathon. Lisa used elements of the AIMS programme in her build-up to Seoul. Her approach was clear. For a marathon race lasting two and a half hours, she would use associative strategies for 95 per cent of the race. Depending on the circumstances, she might not use them for the first and the last mile, but apart from those she would use an associative focus.

During a normal training week she might be on the roads for many hours, and she could cover in excess of a hundred miles. During certain passages of her training she might use dissociative strategies, as she was just 'clocking up the miles'. Within reason, on some of her longer, slower sessions it did not matter what she focused on. But what was of interest was that even on some of these duller sessions she would still use certain sections of the run to practice locking into associative thinking. She had worked out for herself that she could not get into the habit of dissociative thinking exclusively in case this made it hard for her to use associative thinking when it came to racing.

Accordingly, based in part upon Lisa's experiences, the advice now is to use associative for racing and some training, and use dissociative only for training. **Figure 17** is included here to illustrate some dissociative techniques or topics but there are many variations on this theme.

1. Counting: count the number of red cars, Fords, trees, speed limit signs, people.
2. Sporting great: play the role of an athlete you really admire when he or she is achieving some spectacular feat.
3. Instant wealth: decide how would spend your Lottery winnings.
4. Anti-establishment: pretend that you are finally in a position to tell the boss, teacher or some hated figure of authority where to get off.
5. Colours: spend time focusing on the colours that you see while exercising.
6.Debate: try to argue successfully for both sides on a controversial issue.
7. School days: relive an experience with your closest friend at school.
8. Musical performer: see yourself as a rock musician or a virtuoso performer on a stage at a major concert.
9. Tourist: try to recall some of the places you have visited or family holidays.
10. Alphabet game: choose a category, such as countries or people's names and then work through the alphabet thinking of one example for each letter.
11. Music trivia: pick a musician or group and try to recall all of their hits or albums; can you remember any of the lyrics?
12. Different job: try to imagine yourself doing a completely different job or fulfilling a different role.

Fig 17

CHAPTER SIX

Judging Performance

He who excuses himself accuses himself.
William Shakespeare

Athletes frequently form attributions for the success and failure they experience in sport. These attributions determine expectations and emotions which may affect future behaviour. Athletes at all levels experience both successes and failures. Most athletes can accept the inevitability of this situation. As young athletes progress they are bound to be exposed to a range of competition, and hence they experience a variety of results. This is a natural and normal part of sport. However, it appears that there are important differences concerning the ways in which athletes react to success or failure.

This area of sport psychology includes a theory known as Attribution Theory and it looks at the way athletes attribute their successes and failures to internal factors (things that they control) or external factors (things that other people control). This has previously been referred to as Locus of Causality (Weiner, 1979). Athletes who are prepared to accept responsibility for their performance when they win, but who want to blame others when they lose are guilty of using something known as Self-Serving Bias. They are happy to internalize success, but they want to externalize failure.

Coaches, friends and loved ones can play a vital role in helping athletes to develop a healthy attitude towards performance. Athletes should be encouraged to accept responsibility for both success and failure. If an athlete does well in a competition it should be perfectly acceptable to say 'Yes, I deserved this victory because I trained hard and I put in the effort.' Coaches should actively encourage this type of positive attitude. But if an athlete under achieves in a similar event he should still be able to accept responsibility. How many times have you heard competitors complain about the weather conditions or their footwear or the journey to the venue? Athletes should be encouraged to accept that certain elements of any poor performance are due to their own efforts.

In the Seoul Olympics in 1988, the American middle-distance star Johnny Gray performed badly in a race and failed to win a medal. On arriving at the Games he was a favourite for a medal and his world ranking suggested that he might even get a gold. In a press conference after the event he launched into a tirade of abuse against the Korean organizers.

As was the norm for any Olympic track race, the athletes were marshalled together some 30–40 minutes before the start. They all sat in a 'holding' room and awaited instructions to go out on to the main track.

In his press conference Gray said that it was inhuman to be held waiting in these conditions and that this did not happen on the professional circuit. He said that he would have won the race if it had been a normal, one-off event on the circuit. Clearly he used the pre-race conditions as an excuse for his failure, even though the conditions were the same for all the competitors. He had externalized the reasons for his failure.

In Atlanta in 1996, Igor Tradenkov won the silver medal in the pole vault. In the press conference afterwards he bemoaned his luck and complained about the competition having taken far too long (there was a delay after one of the uprights broke), about the airline who had lost his poles a week before the Games, about his wife being disqualified from her event, about the heat and humidity, and about the fact that his great rival Sergei Bubka was injured and therefore the 'tag' of favourite fell to him instead. Not once did he mention anything that he could have done better himself.

Similar examples may be gleaned from reading the newspapers on a Monday in Britain during the football season. Invariably there is a club manager blaming the referee for the fact that his team had lost. There is almost a sub-culture which says that it is acceptable to put the blame on referees within football. The tennis coverage during the Wimbledon fortnight also offers many examples of players who lose and then complain about some external factor which led to their downfall. This happens especially in the first week if one or more of the favoured, seeded players lose.

Athletes within the AIMS programme are encouraged to take the view that sport is like a 'do-it-yourself' project. You take both the applause and the criticism. If they do a good job it is down to them. If they do a bad job it is also down to them. We say 'The day you take complete responsibility for yourself, the day you stop making excuses, that's the day you start your journey to the top.' We might add to this and say, 'There is no such thing as bad weather, just soft athletes.' Athletes on the AIMS programme are encouraged to say 'The problem is mine – I own it.'

Attribution theory also focuses on stability and controllability. The stability dimension refers to whether causes are stable or unstable over time, while controllability refers to whether causes are controllable or uncontrollable.

Within the AIMS programme athletes are encouraged to evaluate all aspects of their performances, irrespective of the results. A judgemental response might oversimplify things: 'I was great today', or 'I was rubbish out there today.' Neither of these responses is likely to help to point the way forward for the next competition. By comparison, athletes following the AIMS programme are encouraged to take a far more analytical view of their performances. They must learn to review things in a comprehensive manner. This is not to say that they should not be allowed to make mistakes along the way. Athletes are told that they should be prepared to make mistakes, because if they do not they are not growing as athletes.

This is also the approach adopted by Tony Pickard, the coach to the tennis star Stefan Edberg. He wants each match to be evaluated promptly after the conclusion. 'We discuss things straightaway, whether it is a win or a loss, and then we are finished with it. Once it has happened it's history. It's no good harping on it. If we won every time I would not learn one goddamned thing.'

Figure 18 is an example of a post-match evaluation sheet used with the Australian women's hockey team from 1987 onwards. It is a variation of the Training Evaluation Sheet (**Figure 10** in Chapter One).

Australian Women's Hockey Squad 1987 Match Evaluation Sheet

Date.....................*Opposition*......................................*Score*...................

Venue..*Playing Position* ....

Rate on a five-point scale:

1 = the pits!
2 = below average
3 = average
4 = above average
5 = very good

Pre-match 'appetite'	1 2 3 4 5
'Tuning-in' ability	1 2 3 4 5
Quality of warm-up	1 2 3 4 5
Concentration capacity	1 2 3 4 5
Quality of warm-down	1 2 3 4 5
Feeling after match	1 2 3 4 5

Which two aspects of the match were you most happy with?

1.
2.

Which features of the match were you least happy with?

1.
2.

Any other general comments?

Fig 18

In a similar way to the Training Evaluation Sheet, the players were being asked to stop and think about many elements of their performance. They were, for instance, even asked to assess the quality of their warm-down. The players took this exercise seriously. This team won the gold medal in Seoul in 1988 when they beat the home side 2–0 in the final. Understandably the team was very happy and there was much celebration after the final whistle. What was interesting, however, was that in the period in between the whistle and then receiving their gold medals (some 30 minutes) several of the players went to the trouble of filling in their Match Evaluation Sheets. The tournament was over but one of the players said (perhaps a little tongue in cheek) that they were already preparing for their next match and the sheet was a way of reminding them why and how they had won the gold medal.

The Match Evaluation Sheet is a way of emphasizing to the players that they must accept responsibility for their own actions and performances. The items which have to be ranked on the sheet are all elements which are within their control. They have to accept ownership of these factors and assess themselves as objectively as possible.

Clearly, the nature of sport is such that on occasions there will be elements of luck which may work for or against any athlete. Over time these should balance out. Athletes are human beings and obviously they are entitled to feel upset when some stroke of luck works against them. They may even say some things in the heat of the battle which suggest that they are externally attributing failure. But what is most important within the AIMS programme is that the athletes themselves know the true score. They are able to focus on evaluating performance, all aspects of it. The result of a hockey match may have turned on one umpiring decision, but there will be many other elements of an athlete's performance which can still be evaluated. The athlete learns to judge his performance on many levels – not just the result – and much of the emphasis is on evaluating factors within the athlete's control.

CHAPTER SEVEN

Psychology of the Olympic Games

It's all about handling the village life – dealing with all that spare time. You have to stay focused and avoid overtraining. You have to manage the time and get on with life as usual.

Wilf O'Reilly, British speed skater

The pressure at the Games is constant – day after day. It's like a tourniquet. The closer it got the harder it was to relax.

Steve Scott, American track athlete

It's very easy, when you are living in the village, to get distracted by everything that is going on around you. When you're staying in the village for a week or more before you compete, it is very easy for you to become too caught up in the atmosphere and emotion of the Games very early on, and I think this is detrimental to your attitude and your performance on the day.

Rob De Castella, Australian marathoner

The Olympic Games are unique. They are also uniquely stressful. In the entire history of the Games there have only been about 5,000 British competitors, and only about 400 Britons have ever won gold medals. Many elite athletes, including former stars, such as Geoff Capes and David Bedford, have returned from the Olympics with their dreams shattered, complaining that no one had prepared them for the nature of the experience.

Experienced Olympic observers also take the view that each successive Games is getting more and more challenging. Each one is just a little tougher than the preceding one . As mentioned in Chapter Five, the American sport psychologist Bob Nideffer is a well-rounded, experienced individual. He is not a man prone to histrionics or exaggeration. Therefore his comments, made when he returned to the USA after accompanying the national track and field team in the 1988 Seoul Olympics, make quite worrying reading. His words were addressed to an audience of fellow sport psychologists:

I spent a great deal of my time trying to help athletes and coaches cope with the pressures created by sponsors, athletes' agents and the media. Team coaches we had were threatened with law suits, and [we] had individuals threaten to 'ruin their coaching careers'. Everyone from personal coaches, to agents representing athletes, to various administrative officials, to newspaper reporters, and even politicians wanted to tell the staff how to do their job. Caught in the middle of all of this were the athletes. There were times when athletes threatened coaches and administrators literally with their lives, and times when 'team members' and their representatives attempted to intimidate other team members. All of this in response to the pressure created by the potential that success at an Olympic level promises from an economic perspective.

I felt that there was a rather dramatic increase in the level of psychopathology that we saw at the 1988 games, relative to 1984. I saw much more hostility, and higher levels of mistrust. I honestly believe a great deal of that can be attributed to increased usage of steroids. We saw athletes who were hallucinating, and athletes who were threatening either suicide or homicide. As you might imagine, it wasn't too difficult for athletes to become distracted and/or to make excuses for their own negative thinking and/or low levels of self-confidence. For the most part, it was negative thinking, anger and self-doubts that I found myself trying to help everyone cope with.

So what is so special about the Olympics that might have caused this situation in Seoul? There are major events or championships every year in most sports. It varies from sport to sport, but these could include world championships and European championships. However, these events are typically single-sport events where all of the competitors are rowers, shooters or hockey players. But the Olympics are quite different. Clearly the sporting event itself is like any normal world championships, but it is taking place within the context of a much bigger, multi-sport festival. This is a unique setting and it presents many new challenges to the athletes and officials associated with the Olympic preparation. The sport psychologist's role is to help to prepare everyone for dealing with the unexpected, and this is especially true when dealing with athletes who are about to make their Olympic debut.

Having attended four separate Olympic Games, I may say with some confidence that each Games is unique. Each includes some element that is unexpected, and the only thing that can be predicted is that the athletes will be faced with something that is unexpected. The AIMS programme was designed to assist athletes and their coaches to cope with the unexpected at the Games. The Olympic Games are like a jeweller's polishing machine. Depending on what the athlete is made of, the machine either makes him shine and glitter, or more often than not, it simply grinds him down. If the athlete is a real gem then things go well and he looks great, but if he is a fake, then he is in trouble.

To be successful in the Olympics, athletes need to have three 'bones'. The first of these is the *wish* bone. Every athlete needs to come to the Games with a goal in mind. He should be aspiring to something special and this is the wish bone. Many athletes get to go to only one Olympics and it would be a great loss if they wasted the opportunity by not aiming high enough.

The second bone is the *funny* bone. There will be defining moments during the Games when something will go wrong, or something unusual will happen. It is important that the athletes can retain their sense of humour. They have to be able to look at the 'bigger picture' and keep a sense of perspective. They need to be able to enjoy themselves. Typically, they have trained for a minimum of eight years in order to get there, and a great many people would give a great deal to trade places with them for this all-important, three-week period. Some athletes almost feel obliged to go around with a frown on their face to prove that they are taking the Olympics seriously. The AIMS programme teaches athletes that it is acceptable to have fun and that they are allowed to enjoy themselves.

The final bone is the *back* bone. Invariably, there is some sort of crisis during the Games. There is a setback of some description. During these moments the athletes (and, for that matter, the officials too) need significant amounts of intestinal fortitude. They will have to 'guts it out' or return home as very disappointed athletes. One or more of their opponents will display this back bone and so if they wish to compete at this level, then so will they. I take the approach that if someone makes a mistake, three things have to happen: he should admit it, learn from it and not do it again. This is having backbone.

As well as asking athletes to bring their three bones with them, the AIMS programme also suggests that it is important to have the athlete (and coach) keep their focus on the here and now. The athletes have to live their lives at the Games in the present tense. This is important for a number of reasons, not the least of which is that it helps the athletes to focus in on things that they can control. Time seems both to speed up and slow down during the Games and many athletes talk about a time distortion effect while in the village in particular. Albert Einstein once said, 'I never think of the future – it comes soon enough.'

In any given Olympic campaign there are various factors which are uncontrollable, for example: which of the opposition are fit and healthy, who is injured, and what decisions the referees and umpires will make. By definition, these factors are beyond the control of the athletes and hence there is little point in worrying about them. By comparison, there are a number of controllable factors, such as an athlete's own attitude to training, nutrition and discipline. The focus of attention naturally has to go towards the controllable factors.

By asking the athletes to 'chunk' their time at the Games into manageable pieces they are much less likely to become distracted by uncontrollable factors. In addition, they are more likely to manage their time more appropriately and have fewer problems with boredom in the village.

The 'here and now' principle would dictate to an athlete that if he is currently in the dining hall for a meal, then this is exactly what he should be focusing on. For instance, he is probably making sure he keeps up his fluid levels and eats the correct types of food. If the next item on his itinerary is a training session, then not surprisingly he focuses his mind on that while actually doing it. If his next appointment is with the physio-therapist, then he concentrates on that while at the clinic. He should be able to go through his day concentrating on the right thing at the correct time. This is not to say that he is not allowed to relax and enjoy himself, but it is to say that he does not just aimlessly drift through the day with little purpose.

If athletes do not retain this present-tense focus then they can do one of two things which may be counter-productive. They either spend too much time dwelling on the past (and given the problems with self-doubt at this stage of preparations this is not very useful), or they start trying to predict the future and too much time is spent worrying about what might lie in front of them. For example, they may have one less than perfect training session and then are unnerved about things which might go wrong for them when they do eventually compete. In any given period an athlete will have his or her best and worst training session. The trick is to make even the worst session fairly good; but it cannot be denied that at some stage a session will not go to plan. By encouraging athletes to live in the here and now they are more likely to be able to complete the session, analyse it, learn from it, but then put it to bed because it is history and cannot be changed. They then move on to the next time slot which might be having a massage or a team briefing or simply having a sleep.

In 1984 David Ottley won a silver medal in Los Angeles in the javelin event. In an interview that followed this performance he recalled the advice given to him by his coach Frank Dick after competing well in the qualifying competition the day before the final. He was told to go back to the village and forget about the competition he had competed in that day. It was past and it could have no bearing on the final. He was told to focus on the things he could control between then and the final. He was not to get carried away by his encouraging qualifying performance. The preparation for the final had already started. Clearly the athlete and the coach were sticking closely to the here and now principle.

In the 1996 women's hockey tournament in the Atlanta Games, Great Britain started poorly. Although they were bronze medalists from 1992, they were beaten by the Korean team 5–0 in the opening match. This was a big shock to the team and the entire tournament could have been a disaster from that moment onwards. One day later the British team earned a draw against the favoured Dutch team and this was the start of a series of good results for the British. Many observers were surprised by the Britons' ability to fight their way back.

In the press conference after that match, Jill Atkins, the team captain, said:

> We obviously had an important debriefing after the Korean match. Tonight's performance shows that we were not dwelling on the Korean score. We kept focusing on the present tense, did some good work on the ball and came through strongly. We had to forget about yesterday's match.

It's not easy to work under these hot conditions, especially after a second match in 24 hours.

Another important principle for gaining success at the Games relates to the magical and mythical 'form book'. This book is the one that includes statements such as 'in theory, the Germans should win this event and we are ranked about seventh', 'on paper we are destined to get a bronze medal behind the Dutch and the Americans', 'by rights, we'll make it through to the final but then it'll be tough', and 'we deserve to make the last eight based upon our form before the Games'. This book spells trouble. It either breeds complacency or more likely it may breed a view that there is some sort of hierarchy that is destined not to be upset during the Games. In either event the form book should be burned before the Games.

Dr Roslyn Carbon is a sports medicine specialist who has worked with both the British and the Australian hockey team as well as with the English and the Australian netball team. While her comments refer mainly to team sports, they are nevertheless pertinent to all events. She comments,

> My experience has shown that the form book can be torn up once you enter the gates of an Olympic village. The Olympic hockey matches are not respecters of any ranking system. The pressure means that any team can beat any team. All three medal winning teams in the Barcelona women's tournament were 'underdogs' before the first whistle being blown.

As well as referring to the three bones, the here and now and tearing up the form book, the AIMS programme includes something that is relatively rare in the world of sport psychology – namely, the use of a Risk Register. This is a tool that allows the athletes and coaching staff to predict weeks in advance some of the risks associated with the Games. The AIMS programme includes an approach known as Comprehensive Risk Management and is designed to prepare athletes for some of the hurdles likely to face them during the Games.

Typically, the psychologist leads the athlete or athletes through a session of brain-storming focusing on where the risks will come from. Having done that, he then tries to quantify these risks in terms of both probability and impact. In other words, how likely it is that any given risk will occur and, if it does, what is the potential impact on the athlete's campaign. **Figure 19** is an example of a risk register.

Risk	Probability	Impact	Result
Transport	0.5	0.9	0.45
Heat and humidity	0.8	0.7	0.56
Illness in team	0.5	0.7	0.35

Fig 19.

The probability score is multiplied by the impact score to get a resultant figure. The numbers will always be in the range 0.0–1.0. Any resultant score above 0.4 is something that warrants further attention. In the Comprehensive Risk Management programme such a score then necessitates the planning of some contingency strategy. It is as if the athletes were saying this is a likely risk which will materialize during the Games and so they want a strategy in place before its actually happening. Comprehensive risk management is not a negative nor depressing exercise. On the contrary, it is all about developing confidence and knowing that the athletes can cope. Some examples are outlined below.

Risk Factors at the Olympics

'Tourists'

Unfortunately, in any given Games there will be a number of competitors who have little or no chance of competing for positions in the finals. This is inevitable, but it does not preclude their possible success in the future.

However, there will be another group of athletes (thankfully a relatively small one) for whom actually arriving at the Games represents the summit of their sporting ambitions. This by itself is not a problem, provided that their own level of discipline and focus does not drop so low that they have an adverse effect on other athletes. These competitors can normally be identified in the first few hours or days in the village. Their focus seems to lock on to other, non-task-oriented activities which have nothing to do with their own preparation. Typical distractions could include rushing off to shopping malls in search of Olympic mementos or going off in search of the key competitors such as Carl Lewis or Steffi Graf.

Jon Clark was the assistant coach with the British women's hockey team which won the bronze medal in 1992. He subsequently became the coach to the American men's hockey team for the Atlanta Games of 1996. His American team did not play particularly well and he commented at a press conference, 'We have six or seven players who are still in a dream. They are living the "Olympic moment". Unfortunately, they have been tourists in the Olympic village. They needed to be much more focused.'

'Tourists' may themselves become a distraction to other athletes, and therefore they need to be avoided where possible. However, the accommodation at most Olympics is fairly tight and it is not always possible to avoid them. There have been problems when one set of athletes have finished their own competition but their subsequent behaviour (noise, keeping late nights, for instance) begins to unsettle athletes who are still competing.

Info '96

This was the electronic mail system which was based in Atlanta during the Games. It proved to be useful in keeping competitors and officials up-to-date with what was happening in all sports. It contained results, schedules, quotable material from press conferences and biographical details on all the accredited competitors. It also contained a messaging system and this is where some problems occurred. Certainly experiences at the Games in Albertville, Barcelona and Lillehammer suggest that this facility is both useful (it helps to pass the time of day) and dangerous (it may cause enormous problems if it gets out of hand).

The difficulties arise when some competitors start to 'borrow' colleagues' passwords and then send fictitious messages to others. These may be amusing or offensive. What starts out as casual fun may quickly turn into a serious problem, and in Barcelona in 1992 there was an ugly scene between a group of British athletes due to a 'prank' getting out of hand.

Computer-based Games

The well-prepared athlete plans ahead to deal with the free time available in the village. A common outlet is the use of computer games, but unfortunately some of these may cause problems if played to excess. Some athletes have virtually become hooked on games and spend too much time playing them when they should be resting or sleeping. Worse still, athletes have reported having nightmares from playing certain games too often or too competitively.

First-week Wobbles

For some of the sports, the Games may be divided into three sections: the first week (before any competitions have started, but the athletes are based in the village to acclimatize to the surroundings); the second week (which typically includes the first competitions for many sports); and the third week when the village takes on a different atmosphere as many competitors actually start to leave town. The first week is arguably the most nerve-wracking and certainly the village itself is filled with much tension and apprehension. However, it is also a time of great excitement. As yet no one has actually failed and therefore people might also seem a little optimistic.

But during this week the competitors may also be faced with a sudden and unexpected loss of self-confidence. This outlook may have nothing to do with objective feedback such as recent results or indicators from training sessions. Instead the loss of confidence may simply come from the expectation and pressure associated with being in the final countdown of a campaign that has typically lasted for four years or more.

The excitement of an Olympic Opening Ceremony, as experienced by the British women's hockey team in Atlanta in 1996.

The successful British rowing coach Miles Forbes-Hamilton says that the athletes change during this period before the 'off'. He describes it as the athletes going into 'transmit only' mode. They are still very willing to talk, but they are no longer listening.

Queuing

Some significant former Olympians have written about the Games as simply being one long queue followed by another, even longer one. The first of these may start at the airport check-in and then proceeds through the accreditation process, access to the village, dining halls, telephones, buses to venues, re-entry to the village after training and so on. By themselves, none of these should be enough to worry any experienced athlete. Unfortunately, there may often be some bizarre accumulative effect and a minority of competitors change their behaviours (such as skipping meals) just to avoid the interminable queues.

Dining Halls and Food

The dining halls have become the social centre of the Olympic villages. Athletes will have a lot of time on their hands and there is a temptation to spend an abnormal amount of time in there. This may present problems to those athletes who have a tendency to 'snack' on fast food or inappropriate food. It is an easy habit to fall into – staying longer in the dining hall to see what famous people come in, and at the same time eating another dessert and having another coffee. This is especially worrying if the athlete is 'tapering' and doing virtually no hard training to burn off any excess of calories.

The dining halls themselves typically cater for several thousand diners at any one time, and the resultant noise and commotion may be somewhat off-putting. Many former Olympians have commented that they really wanted to get away from crowds at the Games. Unfortunately, that is impossible in an Olympic dining hall. Shane Gould, the successful Australian swimmer said, 'I coped with stress by playing cards, getting totally involved in a book, or retreating to a quiet place on my own. If none of these worked, such as at the Munich Olympics, I'd eat. In Munich I ate too much and was two or three kilos over my normal weight.'

Media

It seems as if there will be more of the media at every Olympic Games. This represents both a threat and an opportunity for many sports, and each will adopt its own policy for the Games. So-called 'minority' sports enjoy the spotlight which they find only once every four years. However, experience says that the inexperienced competitor or official can find the

Jane Flemming, complete with media interest after winning a second gold medal in Auckland in 1990.

exposure to the media quite daunting. It is all too easy to say something that is misconstrued and suddenly a controversy has started. This is a particular problem in the first week, when the competition has yet to start and the media have little news to write about. Invariably they are looking for something sensational.

Another consideration for some sports is to adopt a policy concerning such ideas as whether or not the competitors should have access to press clippings in the village and how should the 'star' athlete syndrome be dealt with. For instance, in the Seoul Olympics of 1988, Brian Glencross coached the Australian women's hockey team to a gold medal. During the time spent in the village he forbade the players from reading any of the press clippings which would arrive every day at the team headquarters. He reasoned that the comments made by the press were an uncontrollable factor. They might say something positive and useful for his players to read, but then they might not. Accordingly he was not prepared to take the risk and, after consultation with the players, he banned the press clippings.

Similarly, Steve Gunn coached the British coxless four to a bronze medal in the 1996 Games in Atlanta. Johnny and Greg Searle were members of this boat, and they had previously won gold medals in Barcelona in a coxed pair with Garry Herbert in 1992. Steve reasoned that the media would have an understandable interest in the Searle brothers at Atlanta, and so discussed this with the other athletes in the boat, Rupert Obholzer and Tim Foster. The crew planned a strategy for what would happen if the media focused exclusively on the Searles and ignored the other members of the crew. Thankfully they were able to deal with the situation and avoid any consequential sources of stress.

Family and Friends

The role of family and friends at the Olympic Games is not to be underestimated. Generally speaking, family members do not get access to the Olympic village. Many teams are used to travelling around the world fairly isolated from loved ones. If parents and friends appear on the scene only once every four years then this may cause problems. There are many anecdotes concerning athletes missing team meetings or training sessions because they were waiting to meet their familes somewhere outside the village.

Normally these stories relate to the forlorn search for tickets for loved ones. Family and friends are another uncontrollable factor, and the team management is well advised to discuss contingencies before any problems surface. That is not to say that families should be banned from being in the same city as the athletes, but it does mean that guidelines need to be discussed in advance.

Dr Shane Murphy was formerly the chief psychologist at the USA's

Olympic Training Center. He attended several games with the American team. Shane and I met socially in Albertville during the Winter Olympics of 1992. He was having problems with the morale of some of the American team at the Games. Well-meaning sponsors of the team had arranged for a hundred family members to fly out to France. There were many more than this number of parents who wanted to be at the Games and so a draw was held. This was a good idea, except that it made those athletes whose family members were unsuccessful in the draw feel even worse to see other parents at the Games. The result was that there were a fair number of homesick or lonely competitors within the American team.

Families and friends can obviously have an impact even when they are not actually in the same city. An incident in Atlanta springs to mind. There was a piece of poorly judged and inaccurate tabloid journalism in the days before the Games began. On a quiet news day, a journalist wrote that the British team in both Atlanta and the warm-weather holding camp in Florida were under special protection because there had been an IRA bomb threat against them. This made front-page news at home, and not surprisingly there were a number of distressed loved ones telephoning to get reassurance from the athletes and officials. For a day the preparation of some teams and individuals was quite severely disrupted.

Boredom and Sleep

Many athletes will find that their training volume has reduced significantly by the time they arrive in an Olympic village. They will have spare time on their hands and for some competitors this is a major threat. It is certainly something that can be planned for and avoided.

In a similar vein, athletes have to prepare for the possibility of sleep problems. Changes in the environment, small bedrooms, noisy foreigners or compatriots from other sports – these may all adversely affect sleep patterns. Similarly, if athletes spend too much time in their rooms during the day, they will find that the bed will dominate the room and that they will be sleeping during the day. This is fine if they are used to this style of living, but it may cause problems if they are not. They might find it even harder to sleep at night if they have catnapped during the day. As mentioned previously, athletes may become quite emotional and irrational at the Games, and if they are not sleeping well they are likely to get even more disturbed about the situation.

Steve Ovett, Olympic champion middle-distance runner, once said,

> Getting the right balance between training, eating, sleeping and socializing is very difficult in those last few days. You must not get into the habit of doing too much sleeping during the day. The bed tends to dominate the room and it's too easy to simply lie down and have a nap during the day. Then you can't sleep at night.

Linford Christie, Olympic champion sprinter, has stated that

> The night before the final in Seoul, I went to bed about midnight. I believe
> in going to bed when you are really tired, not when you think you should.
> Then you usually lie there just staring at the ceiling, thinking about every-
> thing that could go wrong.

Tim Foster, rowing medalist in Atlanta, described how he had little sleep before one of the early races in the Olympic regatta:

> We got the 5.45 a.m. bus; the only trouble was that we'd been up until late
> because our compound is next door to the water polo venue, and after the
> USA had played last night we had an hour of the Spin Doctors blaring out
> on the tannoy.

Dilution Effect

Most Olympians are familiar with this effect. Most sports have their own world championships but few are multi-sport festivals. The dilution effect brings with it loss of focus and distractions. New temptations are presented to the athletes, and it is easy for teams or squads to get weakened by the whole process. On a 'normal' tour the team are virtually forced to spend time with each other. But at the Olympic Games it is easy to wander off and explore more interesting things. This may lead to disharmony within the team.

In 1988 in Seoul the Australian men's hockey team experienced this to a small degree when a training session took place with fifteen players instead of sixteen because one had gone off to watch a gymnastics session and had forgotten about the planned training session. Robert Clift, a British Olympic hockey champion, commented,

> When the pressure really hit us, we became stronger as a team. Yes, we had
> arguments, but we all wanted to achieve the same thing – success! We sim-
> ply had to remind ourselves that this was basically just another hockey tour-
> nament where the world's best teams were playing. Nothing else, nothing
> complicated – just hockey matches.

'Bit Player'

Some athletes have talked about the Olympics as being a very negative experience. A common concern is that they feel like they are merely 'bit players' who are being manipulated by the International Olympic Committee and the organizers. This may obviously be quite an extreme response and it may easily distract competitors. If anything, the athletes should use this to their advantage and simply focus on the job at hand rather than on any extraneous concerns.

VIPs and Functions

It might surprise some people, but often competitors may be quite happy to meet VIPs and go to functions. Some of this may be explained by boredom, but certainly some of it comes from a sense of having an Olympic 'experience'. These meetings and events may be used effectively therefore in team preparation, but obviously a sense of perspective needs to be maintained. There are many such events open to athletes, but obviously common sense suggests that the athletes should not go off and sample too many new experiences at the most important competition of their lives. Most athletes at the Games have busy programmes to fulfil with their own sport's timetable and hence competitors have to be careful in this regard.

Big Name Competitors

Even some of the most experienced competitors have been known to go celebrity spotting in the village. Again, in moderation this is not a major problem but it is a little bizarre when all Olympians should rightly be regarding themselves as 'stars'. Nevertheless, star spotting does happen and athletes have to be warned about it in advance. The athletes need to see themselves as being 'special' and they need to focus on their own requirements, not those of the stars from the high-profile events.

Security and Transport

These two factors are now omnipresent at Olympic Games and some athletes will get quite irritated or upset by them. The Atlanta Games were particularly poor with regard to transport, and there were at least two 'sit-ins' by athletes in protest against the inadequate service provided by the organizers. Athletes have a low tolerance threshold at this stage of their preparation and this contributes to some significant problems. They are particularly scathing when it comes to organizational incompetence and this may often lead to frustration, rudeness or, in extreme cases, violence.

Linford Christie has said, 'The Games had been physically and emotionally draining for everyone. It had been hot and wearing and we had been subjected to all the extra Olympic hassle – the constant security checks, both at the stadium and at the village; the ever-present security guards; the journeying to and fro in buses; journalists and television with deadlines to meet'; this complements the remarks of Kathy Cook, the successful British sprinter, 'Some athletes can't cope with the hassles and security at the Games. By the time the gun goes there are quite a few who haven't got a hope. They are so drained by it all, they've got nothing left for the race. They haven't been properly prepared by their coaches.'

In 1988 the American boxer Anthony Hembrick missed his bout at the Seoul Olympics because of a problem with the buses and was hence disqualified. After this great misfortune he said, 'My dream went down so fast. You live it every day. You sleep it. You eat it. You train it. I lost my chance to prove I was the best in the world. It will never come again.'

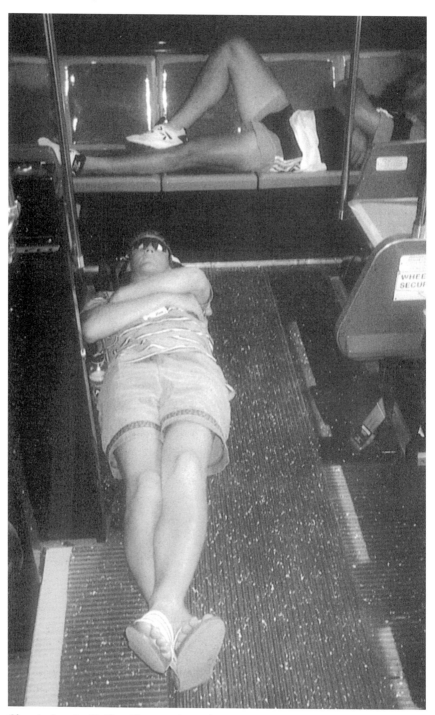

Olympic champion Matthew Pinsent trying to sleep on a bus in Atlanta.

Moving Goalposts

Unfortunately there will be rules and interpretations of rules that change throughout the Games. On the first day a certain class of pass may gain access to a particular area; but by the fourth day the organizers have got their act together or changed their minds and now the pass cannot grant access. This may be frustrating and may have a significant impact if it changes on a competition day when the competitors were assuming the rules to be unchanged. Again, the irritability of the athletes may cause problems in this regard.

Personal Space

Not surprisingly, with 10,000 competitors and only small rooms to sleep in, there is an inevitable sense of having no room in which to unwind when living in an Olympic village. A typical response is to go wandering off for a few hours. This may or may not be significant, depending upon other commitments and obligations. The Olympic bronze medal oarsman Tim Foster said, 'The village was too busy, too noisy and there were too many people in it. To me it was an anti-climax.'

Circus to Workplace Transition

This refers to the all-important ability to switch from the Disneyland environment of the village to the workplace environment of the training or competition site. Athletes will need to be able to make this switch many times during the Games. This is a common problem and, in part, relates to the enormous size of the Games. Some athletes who have a slight loss of form before or during the Games seem to become more easily intoxicated by the whole Olympic process and have more difficulty in being able to make this transition. The Olympic champion oarsman Greg Searle has commented that the trick of coping with the village is not to get infected by all the excitement that is present in the early stages of the Games.

Athletes on the AIMS programme are taught to use the journey away from the village as a punctuation mark. They begin to focus on their own event as they board the bus. This does not mean that they spend the entire journey focusing exclusively on it. For some this would be counter-productive and would serve only to make them more agitated. Nevertheless, they all work out at what stage of the journey they need to 'zoom in' on the event (see Chapter Four).

The athletes are encouraged to have strategies available for dealing with long journeys, if these are to be a regular part of the event. During the 1996 Games many of the rowers had a 75-minute bus journey in each direction to get to the course. The transport problems at the Games made things worse, but it certainly meant that the rowers needed to have plans to cope with the buses. Among the British team the use of 'talking books' of television drama series on audiotapes was quite popular. It was common to see athletes switch off their personal stereos at the same time and at the same spot on the journey, for instance, when the bus turned off the freeway and there were 15 minutes and 10 miles yet to go to the course.

Jay Silvester, former world record holder in the discus, once said,

> The Olympic Games was not my cup of tea, so much pressure, so much anxiety. In my opinion the Olympic villages are a joke. They really are not very good places for athletes to prepare for the greatest competition of their lives. It's like Disneyland: there is an immediate air of excitement as soon as you enter and it's contagious – an Olympic village is the same.

Bedrooms

It is important that people personalize their rooms. The room may become like a prison cell – a very untidy and cluttered place. By taking posters, photographs, games or books the athletes can create a home away from home. The Soviet rooms in Seoul were all very 'decorated'. Triple gold medallist Michelle Smith described her room in Atlanta, 'We had the worst rooms I had ever seen. We had no pillows, and sheets were only just about clean. They were changed once while we were there. The blinds didn't work so we had to tape newspapers on the windows. Even the air conditioning didn't work.'

Walking

Many of us do hardly any walking in our daily lives at home – especially athletes. The village involves a lot of walking, and some athletes may get very tired without realizing it, or they stop going to meals or shops because they are scared of walking too far. In the weeks leading up to the Games, even 'sedentary' athletes should be encouraged to do some walking to prepare for this demand in advance.

To the casual observer it may appear that any athlete or official prepared to put himself through these obstacles and trials must be mad. There can certainly seem to be many pitfalls involved in the event. Nevertheless, as a veteran of four Olympic Games I may say that for the two or three weeks that the Games are on there is no more exciting place to be on the entire planet. Yes, there are trials and tribulations, but there are also special moments which remind you just how fortunate you have been to be involved at all. These moments do not relate only to the joy of being at the opening ceremony or a medal ceremony; they may be of a more minor significance than that.

A most vivid memory I have from Seoul in 1988 took place away from the cameras and the excitement of the Olympic village or the competition sites. The judo teams were allotted different training gymnasia around the Korean capital. I was with the Australian team and we shared a school gymnasium with the Soviet and the Yugoslav team. Australia were not a particularly strong team, but our co-inhabitants were quite a force in world judo. The Australian team would often warm up by playing chasing games such as 'he' or 'off-ground touch'. On one occasion the entire Australian contingent (including the coach, the manager and the psychologist) were involved in this light-hearted warm-up. Our international friends carried on with their more sombre approach and looked over at us as if we were mad or juvenile or both. Some of our bolder judo players dared to run in and around the Soviet and the Yugoslav players and used them as shields from their pursuers. But they were careful not to bump into anyone!

After a few minutes the game was coming to an end, but for some reason one of the braver Australians who was 'it' went up and stood in front of a Russian who weighed about 120kg. The big man stared at the Australian, and then for some inexplicable reason the Australian touched the Russian, said, 'You're "it"!' and then ran off. It was like a moment from a Tom and Jerry cartoon. There was a loud, collective, sharp intake of breath and we all thought that our team-mate would now be killed. Instead the Russian laughed and joined in with the game. This was the signal for all of the thirty or so people in the gymnasium to join in. For about ten minutes there was a hilarious game of multi-lingual 'off-ground touch' and it became apparent that our international friends had been wanting to play these games all week. At that time the Iron Curtain was still in place, and it made this activity all the more remarkable. There have been many similar events and incidents from the Games. They are not the incidents that grab the headlines, but they are some of the ones which leave the most vivid memories.

Conclusion

While this chapter has focused specifically on coping while at the Olympic Games, there is no doubt that the major principles (three bones; 'here and now'; tearing up the form book; and keeping a risk register) apply equally as well to any other major sporting campaign. The AIMS programme has been applied to many non-Olympic events including motor racing, professional heavyweight boxing, world-class squash, professional Rugby League and Union football, international netball and lacrosse, professional darts, professional snooker and professional soccer, to name but some.

Each programme is tailored to the demands of the event or discipline, but the principles remain the same. Each athlete has a bespoke system to work with, but there are many commonalities between the sports. As far as preparation for the big event is concerned, AIMS athletes know that there is a substantial difference between success and failure. It is the difference between doing things nearly right and exactly right. By preparing athletes to face up to the risks and helping them to prepare as thoroughly as possible, the sport psychologist is encouraging them to make the correct decisions throughout the preparation process. The athletes are empowered to take responsibility for their own actions. This is the cornerstone of the AIMS programme.

CHAPTER EIGHT

Team Building

Zvzn though my typzwritzr is an old modzl, it works vzry wzll – zxczpt for onz kzy. You would think that with all thz othzr kzys functioning propzrly onz kzy would hardly be noticzd, but thz onz kzy out of whack szzms to ruin thz wholz zffort.

You may say to yourszlf, 'Wzll, I'm only onz playzr. No one will noticz if I don't do my bzst'. But it dozs makz a diffzrzncz bzcausz to bz zffzctivz a tzam nzzds activz participation by zvzry onz to thz bzst of hzr ability. So thz nzxt timz you think you arz not important rzmzmbzr my old typzwritzr. You arz a kzy playzr...

Many elements of psychological preparation are important in the build-up to an Olympic Games, but when dealing with team sports the AIMS programme tends to concentrate on two major components; developing team cohesion, and empowering individual players. This chapter will be based around an explanation of how these two aspects have been dealt with during Olympic build-up periods or before tours and other tournaments.

Team Cohesion

Social psychologists have analysed the interactions between the individual members of a range of groups. In the last thirty years a great deal of attention has been focused on sporting groups as a source of research data and psychologists all over the world have examined successful teams, squads and clubs in an effort to determine the special factors that influence sporting performance. Group performance has always been a relevant practical issue as many coaches and administrators around the world devote considerable time, effort and money to maximizing team performance.

Group performance always adds the element of interaction among members. According to Shaw (1976), 'A group is defined as two or more persons who are interacting with one another in such a manner that each person influences and is influenced by each other person.'

The degree of interaction may well differ among different sports teams, but it is nevertheless present. In fact, it is this interaction factor that sets apart a group from a mere collection of individuals. Sports groups should be thought of as a collection of interdependent individuals, co-ordinated and orchestrated into a number of task-efficient roles for the purpose of achieving some goal or objective that is deemed important for that particular team.

Models of Group Performance

One conceptual framework was developed by Ivan Steiner (1972) and it has been applied and extended by a number of sport psychologists in the last twenty-five years. The essence of Steiner's theory is that a group's actual productivity is equal to its potential productivity, minus any losses due to faulty process. Actual productivity or performance is what the group actually does. It is the performance that is attained. Potential productivity is the group's best possible performance given its resources and the task demands. The group's resources comprise all relevant knowledge, abilities and skills of the individual members, including the overall level and distribution of these talents.

Process – everything the group does while transforming its resources into performance – is a critical but vague part of Steiner's model. Group processes are the actual steps or actions taken individually or collectively by group members to carry out the group task. When individuals work in groups, communication, co-ordination and interaction are necessary. Process is subdivided by Steiner into two general categories: co-ordination losses and motivation losses.

Steiner's model is classically described using a hypothetical tug-of-war team. In the case of a two-man team, each individual might be capable of pulling 100kg. Thus the potential productivity is 200kg. However in a controlled trial the actual performance is only 180kg. The group has experienced a decrement of 20kg or 10 per cent and this is probably due to the inability of the two athletes to co-ordinate their efforts or because one or both athletes were inclined to let the other do most of the work. The result is the process loss.

This idea of process loss is fundamental to the psychological skills programme developed within AIMS for team sports. When Steiner's model is extended into the competitive arena it becomes obvious that process loss must be reduced. If Team A is to be more effective than Team B then there are three contrasting scenarios that will make this possible; see **Figure 20**.

1.Team A possesses greater relevant resources than Team B, and experiences fewer process losses than the opposition
2.Team A possesses greater relevant resources than Team B, but experiences approximately equal process losses
3.Team A possesses approximately equal relevant resources, but experiences fewer process losses

Fig 20

Clearly the role of the sport psychologist is to work to reduce the amount of process loss that occurs and the AIMS programme focuses on allowing athletes and coaches to ensure that this happens.

At the elite level most of the teams will be fast, strong, powerful, skilful and experienced. Hence a team could not rely on winning the gold medal because of the first or the second scenario in **Figure 20**. During the course of a tournament a team must be capable of winning within the third scenario. In other words, the teams have comparable relevant resources, but the amount of process loss is different. This is one key element to a successful psychological programme with a team or squad.

Developing Team Cohesion

While the research concerning cohesion and performance is somewhat equivocal, there is no doubt that coaches prefer to work with a team that is cohesive and united in purpose. While it is acknowledged that there have been some notable exceptions to the rule, it is generally accepted that sports teams should be cohesive.

This is particularly true with regards to task cohesion. This refers to the amount of cohesion to be found in the 'doing' part of the sport, while social cohesion generally refers to that away from the sporting arena. It is possible to have a successful team which has high levels of task cohesion, yet only moderate levels of social cohesion. Indeed, there have been some very successful teams which contained quite high levels of friction.

When in 1990 the then West German football team won the World Cup their coach Franz Beckenbaur said that some of the success was due to the tightly knit, cohesive squad. He commented, 'In previous squads we would see players sitting down to meals and staying within their club groups. A Munich table here, a Cologne table there. This year it has been different. Everyone mixes in and it makes for a better team.'

The remainder of this chapter will focus on the practical elements associated with developing both types of cohesion within elite sporting groups. All examples have been taken from the AIMS programme.

Post-Game Analysis

If a team is involved in a tournament they will often have to play a number of matches spread over several days. Most World Cups and Olympic competitions are based around such a format. It is important that when one game is completed players and coaches learn from it, discuss the implications of it, and then put that game out of their minds as they prepare for the next encounter. Because that game is over there is no point in worrying about it as the result is already in the record books. It is vital that players are assisted to analyse a performance honestly and accurately. They learn from it, but win, lose or draw, they must not dwell on it.

Although this strategy would be regarded as common sense in the cold light of day, it is easier said than done when the athletes are involved in a vital competition. It is likely that in the face of a disappointment players may be tempted to over-analyse and be overly critical of themselves, their team-mates or the coach. Typically this does not make a positive contribution to subsequent pre-match preparation. It may lead to the development of cliques or disaffected factions within the group.

The Australian women's hockey team became Olympic champions in 1988 having worked with the AIMS programme for 18 months before the Games. They started to use the idea of post-match debriefing sessions in 1987. During these the players were asked a variety of questions. They might be asked to name the thing they were most happy with from their own performance and the one that they were least happy with. Or they might be asked to give one key point about their individual game and one about the team performance. Or perhaps only the forwards or the defenders or the substitutes might be asked for their opinions. Importantly, there was always an opportunity for any player to give her view on any aspect of the game.

Finally, and always at the end of the player input, the coaches would give their thoughts on the match. As part of the empowering coaching style adopted by the two coaches, they thought it important not to stifle any player's contributions by dictating the theme of the meeting with their own observations.

These sessions, known as post-game analysis or PGA, were utilized after every practice game, every test match or every Olympic encounter, irrespective of the result. They allowed the players to 'put the game to bed' and concentrate on the next one. This approach helped to improve task cohesion and reduced the opportunities for any destructive social factors to develop.

The British women's hockey team won the bronze medal in the 1992 Olympic Games in Barcelona. They had also used the AIMS programme for about 18 months before the Games. They also used PGA in their build-up. While the notion of PGA could not be described as revolutionary, it did have a profound effect on the levels of both task and social cohesion within the squad. There was a refreshing amount of honesty within the team, which perhaps had not been present in the early days. The team grew to work by the credo 'we win together or we lose together' – the two important words were 'we' and 'together'.

Sandy Gordon is a Scot who lives in Perth, Western Australia. He has worked as a sport psychologist with many successful individuals and teams. He has coined the post-match debriefing exercise as the four 'Rs' –

Review, Retain, Rest and Return (Gordon 1990). This is a useful variation on the PGA system and is sometimes drawn upon within the AIMS programme. It is simple but quite effective.

Modified Match Practice

Chapter Four included details of how the 1988 Australian women's hockey team played practice matches against a backdrop of crowd noises reproduced over a noisy public address system. As mentioned previously, this was to help to prepare the team for the possibility of playing against the Koreans and a partisan local crowd.

These matches were also used to develop mental toughness and team cohesion. During certain specified passages in the matches a variety of challenges were thrown at the players. Unbeknown to the players, the umpires had been asked to become gradually more and more biased against the Australian team. Also, the opposition (which included six good quality male players) indulged in 'targeting' or 'sledging'. Focusing on one or more of the Australian players they tried either to physically 'rough them up' or verbally single them out for some fairly harsh insults. Initially, some of the players responded poorly to this, but they were forced to adapt and cope. This helped to develop mental toughness and even further enhanced their already strong sense of team spirit.

In addition to these practice matches against 'outside' opposition, many or most training sessions in 1988 would include some sort of small-sided games among themselves. When I was first introduced to them in late 1986, perhaps too much of their training programme was based around skill development. Many of the players trained twice a day as scholarship holders at the Australian Institute of Sport. They were becoming very skilful as individual players.

However, a review of their performances in important Test matches showed that in some of the really hard games some of these skilful players would 'go missing'. The nature of hockey is such that the pitch is quite congested and it is possible for players to run into areas where they are unlikely to be passed to by their colleagues. Some of the most gifted players would have 'quiet' matches while the scores were still close, for example, 0–0 or 1–0. But if the team did manage to get two goals up, then magically these players would flourish and show the marvellous skills that everyone knew they possessed. As a result the team might even go on to win by three or four goals, and everyone (including the coaches) would say how well particular players had performed. I was far from convinced by this assessment and wanted these players to be contributing when the score was 0–0.

Brian Glencross readily agreed to put a strategy into place to help to train all the players to be 'fighters' or 'scrappers'. The idea of playing small-sided games of eight versus eight players within the squad of sixteen was hardly revolutionary. Perhaps the fact that we attached it to virtually every training session was less common. But the main emphasis and hence change was in the variations we employed.

The matches were typically played across the pitch and players were asked to perform in a congested area. The matches would start off as an eight versus eight game. Then for the last 7 minutes, for instance, one player would swap teams to make it seven versus nine. The team with seven would be told that one of their team had been sent off and they were playing against the powerful Dutch. They are 2–1 up with seven minutes to go. They have to fight hard and play well to hang on to this rare victory. The two coaches would umpire the game properly. If the team managed to keep this lead then they were the victors and the losers might have some fairly trivial punishment such as being the ones who had to move the two sets of goal posts back to their correct positions. This added a little extra spice to the matches. Or so we thought.

In actual fact, the players were so mentally and physically exhausted at the end of some of these sessions that they really had to drag themselves up to do anything like move the goal posts or collect the balls. Although the theory was that the victors would justifiably get the reward of going straight off for a shower, the growing team spirit within this group was such that the victors would not allow their colleagues to have this extra workload. They would all join in to complete these chores at the end of the match.

From a management point of view, this was an excellent development. The matches were fiercely competitive and yet at no time did the ferocity ever jeopardize the team's cohesiveness. The gifted, skilful players learned how to fight in these matches.

We used a number of scenarios within these matches. Sometimes the team with the extra player was desperately trying to close a two-goal deficit with 13 minutes left to play. Or perhaps for the final 4 minutes of a session it became 10 versus 6 players. Or perhaps there was a four-player defensive unit, and two sets of six attacking players. The first wave of six would attack the goal and try and score. The defenders would try to keep them out. Once one attack had concluded the next wave would attack. This process might last for 12 minutes. Obviously the attacking units were getting one rest in every two attacks, but the defensive unit received no such luxury. They were under a lot of pressure after about 5 minutes and then they were faced with a reward and punishment situation which typically meant they had to let in no goals.

The coaches developed an array of situations which they thought might replicate some of the pressures associated with Test matches. The players were being asked to put their developing technical skills on trial in a fairly pressurized environment and, at the same time, team unity was being fostered.

Nominal Group Technique

Dr Richard Cox introduced me to the idea of Nominal Group Techniques (NGT) in 1994 and since then they have become an integral part of the AIMS programme. NGT refers to a brain-storming process which allows every member of a team or squad to have his say about any given issue. The rules are simple: a group is asked to think about a situation and come up with different ways of approaching it. Provided that each idea is prefaced with the words 'It would be better if...' then anything is permissible. All opinions are valued by the group. Once the group have come up with an exhaustive list they then vote on how important each of the suggestions is. Eventually they arrive at a hierarchy and this lets everyone know where the attention needs to be focused.

By way of an example, the following letter was sent to all members of the British women's rowing team in the spring of 1996 before going to a training camp in France. It is reproduced here to show the factors identified by the group. This then allows them to prioritize those issues requiring special attention at the training camp.

Dear Oarswoman,
Further to our recent meeting, and as promised, here is a summary of the Top Ten factors you identified as giving room for improvement in 1996. You will recall that these were *your* observations and *you* had a chance to vote for the most pertinent examples of 'It would be better if...'

1. We increased our self-belief
2. We had more confidence in our own ability
3. We had a more positive attitude towards each other
4. We used less negative speak (less whinging in training)
5. We just *did* things (ask fewer questions!)
6. We really focused on the first stroke of each outing
7. We were more cheerful towards our coach
8. We were more relaxed about knowing exactly what was going on when and where
9. We functioned more as a team: helped each other
10. We outlined or redefined our goals

Having gone through this exercise it is now most important that we establish action plans as to how we will make improvements in these areas. Clearly there is some overlap between certain factors (for instance, 5 and 8 have overlap, as do 1 and 2, and 3 and 9) and we need to ensure that we focus on the key components.

Team Meetings

The NGT is one form of team meeting, but there are others. The AIMS programme for team sports is often based around increasing and improving communication within a team. Holding regular team meetings is obviously one vehicle in helping to achieve this. Accordingly, teams on the AIMS programme are encouraged to adopt the following ground rules when having meetings:

1. Always agree on the objective(s) for the meeting before you get down to business
2. Always agree an agenda – what will be discussed when
3. Focus on relevant discussion points and do not get sidetracked
4. Respect other people's views
5. Start on time
6. Hold only one meeting at a time (no side meetings)
7. Be open-minded
8. Record issues for subsequent discussions
9. Record minutes of meeting
10. Summarize any agreements and any subsequent deadlines

As an example of one such team meeting, the notes from a rowing meeting dealing with the topic of developing crew spirit are included here. These come from a meeting of the British men's team in 1996 while at a training camp in Spain:

Developing Crew Spirit

Following on from the meeting in Banyoles, April 1996

1. The development of true crew spirit should be natural – not contrived
2. Be prepared to face adversity together
3. Develop the optimism on a daily basis by doing what is 'right'
4. Reduce or eliminate negative, undermining comments
5. Have faith in your colleagues and trust one another
6. Offer encouragement and support in training
7. Do not share crew 'confidences'
8. Avoid 'wind-up' merchants
9. Have confidence in the total process of preparation
10. View experiences as being positive contributions

The Perfect Player

A good team-building exercise may be based around the idea of the team identifying how the perfect or model player deals with various situations. The following example was used with the English men's hockey team in 1990. This was made up of eight reigning Olympic champions from Seoul in 1988 and eight new players. The team went through this exercise just before a short tour of Oman and Pakistan.

The squad divided into four groups of four. Within each the athletes nominated a spokesman and a 'minute-taker' who would keep notes of their group's discussions. Each group included a mixture of experienced and less experienced players. These groups were allowed 30 minutes in which to come up with their ideas on how the perfect player would react to a number of hypothetical situations. It was important to present the players with situations that were common or at least feasible within their sport. There had to be a sense of realism about the examples, and each was developed in conjunction with the coaching staff of the team.

After the 30-minute period, the four small groups returned to a larger meeting where each issue was discussed in turn, with each spokesman presenting his group's opinions. At the end of this session there had been a great deal of discussion as to what was and was not acceptable behaviour or the strategies for dealing with these situations. A consensus was reached and it was agreed that this was the standard by which the players could justifiably judge one another. In other words, they were to assess themselves against this standard on a regular basis.

The following is an extract from the players' touring diary from the trip in 1990.

The Perfect Hockey Player

These notes are a summary of your thoughts on the subject of how the perfect hockey player might react in a variety of situations. It represents a consensus of how you feel an English international should deal with things that occur around him. While on this tour you will be asked to assess yourself informally as to how well you match up to these criteria. After your matches in Pakistan you can fill in the appropriate page and score yourself, marks out of ten, for any of the items that you think are relevant to you.

Reacts to mistakes by himself : recognizes the mistake, but doesn't dwell on it. That event has finished and cannot be altered now. He takes responsibility for the error, but makes sure that it doesn't affect his next involvement in the game by focusing on the next pass, shot, trap or tackle. He plays each event in the game on its merits, and concentrates on one event at a time.

Handles indifferent umpiring: it's about personal control. The umpire cannot be allowed to become a scapegoat for a player's poor performance. If the umpire interprets a rule in an unusual manner then it is up to the player to adjust for that particular game, in other words, don't keep making the same mistake even if you know that you are in the right. The player has to be able to control his frustration and not become distracted by any one umpire or decision. If this does happen he will need to refocus by spending a minute or two concentrating on the dimples on the ball, or the maker's name on the sticks: on a narrow focus of attention.

Deals with coming on from the bench: there is a need to adapt quickly when coming on from the bench. Players have to be tuned-in throughout the game and this can be achieved by watching specific areas of play rather than simply watching the game as a spectator might. Any warm-up time that becomes available (sometimes there isn't any, of course!) should include both physical and mental preparation. Visualization and reminding yourself of goals and objectives can be helpful. Players should be permanently ready: shinguards, mouthguards, stick, for instance.

Reacts when yellow-carded (temporarily suspended from the game): same as above, only now there is probably a greater emotional element – feel aggrieved. Need to forget about the incident as quickly as possible and concentrate on tactical/technical things occurring in the match. Keep warm, even in hot conditions it is important to stay active: stretching, for instance.

Copes with minor injuries after the game: seeks immediate treatment and advice from doctor and physio. One game is finished and now the focus is on preparation for the next game, therefore it's important to get looked after rather than think about a shower, sleep or the bar.

Reacts to mistakes by team-mate: all international players know when they've made a mistake – no need to shout at them. Any limited criticism needs to be positive and constructive. Players need to be encouraged. If the opposition sense that there is disharmony in the team (as witnessed by verbal or non-verbal reactions) they can exploit it.

Copes with biased crowds: doesn't become intimidated and retains a focus on playing. Tries to use it as a source of positive motivation. If the player becomes distracted he should focus on dimples, names on sticks or the sound of the ball. Be aware of unique problems for wingers and goalkeepers.

Attitude towards training: doesn't cheat himself or the team. Gets tuned-in before arriving at the ground by setting himself goals for each training session. Adopts correct concentration pattern when it's his turn within a given drill, and doesn't use destructive criticism to players or coaches. Maximizes valuable time on the turf, especially during international competitions when this is limited. Training sessions should be relatively short and intensive, but very focused and productive.

Reacts to fluctuations in performance: be able to recognise the source of any problem. Be prepared to seek advice and don't just keep any self-doubts to yourself – especially when overseas. Ask for more detailed advice from coaches and play your way back into form by playing the percentages rather than trying to be the match-winning hero every time. Players also need to remember to wear their 'crap detectors' at times.

('Crap detectors' is an expression which implies that people outside the team, for instance, fans, family or committee members, might be tempted to proffer advice which may not be very useful to the player or team.)

The same session was carried out with the Australian women's hockey team in 1988 and several of the responses were similar. Then, just before leaving for Seoul, the Australian squad divided into small groups and went off to think about their view of the perfect coach. Their verbatim responses are included here as an example of what elite players (who were about to go on to become Olympic champions) wanted from their coaches as the Games approached.

Summary of Perfect Coach Session

1. Media: coach should not use press to embarrass or belittle the team. Always be supportive and be willing to praise players when things have gone well. Not put unnecessary pressure on team. Generally happy with how this is currently handled.

2. Team officials: want any 'blow-ups' to be conducted away from the players. Want all staff to put players' needs ahead of their own.

3. Offering solutions: be big enough to say, 'I don't know', without getting defensive and uptight. Don't be too proud and direct the player to *one* outside source of information for additional advice.

4. What-ifs: be cool and calm. Don't overreact or panic. Coping with defeat is tough. It's worse when the coaches don't say anything after such an event. Be available for individual contact and listen to what is being said.

5. Player input: occasionally ask for player opinion about how training drills, etc. went, and then try to implement these comments.

6. Videotape: not to be shown too late at night. Short and sharp, and preferably specific. Small groups are excellent. If players are watching an entire game, don't keep stopping and asking for replays over and over again. Keep the videotapes positive.

7. Training sessions: be flexible if a drill is not working. Keep sessions short and to the point. Be specific and match-like. Small groups (such as defenders or lefties) are well received. There is too much queuing up at times. Probably need to make defending drills more interesting. More time available for free practice time – worked well early on during training camp in Canberra.

8. Bench-warmers: be equitable and don't ignore them. Talk to them during the game and remain positive.

9. Team selection: pick the best team available for each game and don't ignore the reserves.

10. Providing feedback: players don't like receiving 'nothing'. Criticism is better than nothing. Some players prefer specific stuff while others get confused by this. Coaches should be readily available and, if possible, use video for examples.

(A 'what if' – no. 4 above – is an event or incident which has the potential to disrupt an otherwise stable situation. For instance, a 'what if' might be

British women's hockey team undertaking the 'Perfect Player' exercise in Holland in 1992.

that the team transport fails to turn up on time before a match or the team captain is injured and has to be sent home from a tour.)

A similar session was conducted with the British women's hockey team in both 1992 and 1996. In the class of 1996 the management team was asked individually to identify what they saw as their roles within the 'team' (Olympic hockey teams have sixteen players and typically six or seven management personnel). They each came up with a list. There was some overlap: for instance, some of what the physiotherapist did was also what the team doctor did, and vice versa. These lists were then cut up so that each piece of paper included only one item or role. The pieces were then jumbled up and the players had to identify who was responsible for what within the management team. It turned out to be an amusing session, and in most instances the players were correct. Then, to reciprocate, the players had to work in pairs and come up with their own lists of what the roles and responsibilities of the players were. The resulting list is included here:

The Roles and Responsibilities of a British Hockey Player

Milton Keynes, June 1996

- Follow fitness programme
- Perform to best of ability and get results
- Adhere to injury rehabilitation programme
- Be the owner of the acclimatization process
- Be self-motivated
- Take care of nutrition/hydration
- Stay focused and avoid distractions
- Mentally prepare for each match
- Liaise with management
- Be supportive and tolerant of each other
- Be familiar with the 'drugs in sport' issues and check all medications with the doctor first
- Concentrate and give input during debriefs
- Conform to team decisions
- Selectively listen to advice
- Acquire tactical advice
- Accept criticism
- Have tactical understanding specifically towards set pieces
- Be disciplined with regards to rest and recuperation
- Be organized, prepared and punctual
- Analyse opponents
- Be very goal-oriented

SWOT Techniques

Another useful team building technique is to review a group's SWOT analysis. This technique has been used extensively in the commercial world for many years, and I have used it with elite performers since 1990. The acronym stands for Strengths, Weaknesses, Opportunities and Threats. Again the session is run as a discussion exercise and once the individuals involved have identified the SWOTs they then must explore ways in which they can build on strengths, eliminate weaknesses, exploit opportunities and mitigate the effects of threats. Ideally, the participants will accept responsibility for these elements and then establish action plans as to how they will make progress in these categories.

I have included two examples here. The first comes from the British men's heavyweight coxless four and the second is from the British women's hockey team. In both instances these sessions took place approximately six weeks before the Olympic Games of Atlanta, and in both cases half of the team or crew were already Olympic medalists.

Men's Coxless Four: SWOT Analysis, June 1996

Strengths

Timing of our best effort – we are big-match players
Technically sound
Sensitive to the need to change things
Good confidence in our ability
Good second half of race
We know each other well and we trust each other
Physically strong
Good boat speed relative to rate

Weaknesses

Not quick enough in the first half of the race
Consistency of mental preparation for *all* training sessions
Inconsistency on the water during outings
Some difficulties with communication and not wanting to compromise
Our reaction to adversity may be extreme and a little uncontrolled

Opportunities

We are 'dark horses' and the unknown force in the event
Have high level of confidence in off-water back-up
Make significant progress in the two training camps pre-Atlanta
Exploit our reputation for being tough racers

Threats

Final training camp conditions are far from perfect
Media start to become intrusive
Village issues such as boredom and distractions
Escalation of rows/differences between us
Injury/illness
We get desperate rather than use thoughtful application

British women's hockey team – winners of bronze medals in Barcelona in 1992.

Women's Hockey: SWOT Session, June 1996

Strengths

Pace of attack
Individual flair
Passionate for success
Olympic experience
Goalkeepers
Versatility
Depth
Tenacious
Penalty corners (attacking and defending)
Team spirit
Workrate and physical strength
Agility
Counterattacking
Will to win
Professional management and trainers

Weaknesses

Not honest enough
Concentration in last 5 minutes
Limited flair
Reaction to decisions
Not good in morning matches
Defending penalty corners – second phase

Keeping possession
Vulnerable when winning
Create more penalty corners
More confidence re. finishing in the circle
Inconsistency during the matches
First touch
Lack of self-belief
Lack of objectivity and tolerance of each other
Not intimidatory enough in shooting situations
Inability to focus during 'central' training sessions

Opportunities

Well-respected team
Exploit psychological, physiological and medical opportunities in next 38 days
Acclimatization programme
Been to Atlanta
Establish authority over European opposition
Develop physical presence
Olympic experience
Learning in training sessions
Using trip to North Carolina to get correct balance between work and rest
Exploit opponents' inexperience and nervousness
Exploit tapering programme
Having seven games to play
Exploit weak links in opponents
React positively and promptly to umpires

Threats

Focus – distractions
Village – distractions
Opposition penalty corners
Overtraining, burnout, illness/injuries
Humidity
Complacency
Reaction to unexpected tactics
Hype: transition from village to pitches
Benchwarmers – impact from family and friends who might have expected more
gametime for their loved ones
Media
Not played on Atlanta Pitch1 before
Opposition targeting individual players
Rooming – personal space
Our reaction to verbals
Umpiring
Poor warm-up results
Responding to results in the early part of the competition
USA and Americans re. wave of enthusiasm

Clearly, many of the SWOT elements are highly sport-specific and again
the subtleties are difficult to appreciate if, like me, you are not an expert
in these events. Nevertheless, there are clues to be gleaned from this material concerning the relative priorities of top-class athletes at this tense

stage of their preparation. Both groups, for example, list the media and the distractions of the Olympic village as possible threats. Under weaknesses both groups imply that tolerance of each other may become an issue. These are obviously important clues for coaches, psychologists and management in general.

What If...

Another commonly used technique for team building and contingency planning is known as 'What if...'. The AIMS programme has used it regularly since the early 1980s. It has been found it to be a useful 'bonding' exercise and it may say much about the individuals who go to make up a team or squad.

Normally, various hypothetical situations are preplanned. Many of these are gleaned from stories of real-life events. Typically the team would again be divided into small groups and go off to consider their responses to them and then share their reactions with the whole group. The psychologist, a coach or manager might throw in some additional elements that may have been missed by the athletes, but, by and large, the experienced performers normally have a good idea.

The basic rule taught to these athletes revolves around the acronym of COPE. This implies that when faced with the unexpected, the athlete should Control his emotions, Organize the input (for instance, verify what he is being told), Plan a response, and Execute that plan. By way of example, some 'what ifs' used with another group of netballers going to the Caribbean (again the AIS team but now the class of 1988) have been included, and some examples used with the British Olympic team's management group.

AIS Netball Tour 1988

What if...

1. The bus that is supposed to meet us at the airport does not turn up?
2. The coach gets sick overseas and has to return to Australia?
3. You find that the standard of umpiring is unacceptably low?
4. The weather in the Caribbean is so hot that the quality of training is low?
5. You find that some of the other players are so noisy at night you can't get to sleep?
6. You are playing badly and can't understand why?
7. A local journalist asks you about the standard of accommodation or opposition or food?
8. Someone falsely accuses you of shoplifting and you are arrested?
9. You feel really homesick while you're away?
10. You feel that one or two of the girls are more concerned with being 'tourists'?
11. There is an unexpected 8-hour delay at the Dallas airport?
12. The transport arrangements in Jamaica are inadequate?

13. You are not coping well with spending time on the substitutes' bench?

14. You find that from Day 1 your bodyweight is increasing?

15. The pre-game ceremonies seem to be dragging on and you find yourself distracted?

16. The bus-trip to the game is taking much longer than it should because of traffic problems?

17. You find yourself being 'sucked-in' by a partisan crowd or umpire?

The next examples come from work that had been carried out with the managers from the British Olympic team before the Barcelona Olympics. It should be easy to note that the emphasis in the nature of the 'what ifs...' changes, depending on whether the individual is a performer or a manager.

With one or two minor changes to some of the details, the following are true examples of situations that management teams have faced at previous major championships. You are asked for your opinion on what you would do if faced with these situations. There are no right answers as such, but hopefully there are some general principles that you would apply to these events. Hopefully we can learn from each other's experiences and as a result be better prepared for 1992.

1. You are just finishing off a team meeting and in 10 minutes time you will leave for the competition venue. Suddenly one of your athletes notices that her accreditation pass is incorrect. She has got a Hungarian pass that belongs to another athlete. Your athlete says that there must have been a mix-up at the sauna and spa area in the village centre. Apparently the athletes have to hand in their passes before they go into this facility. They are then given their passes when they leave. Obviously, someone else is wandering around with your athlete's pass around her neck. Another couple of minutes have elapsed while this has been explained to you. The athlete is now getting very agitated, and some of the other team members are also being affected. *What will you do now?*

2. Acting on medical advice, it is obvious that one of your key athletes, who has sustained an injury, has to be sent home from the village. He does not know yet, and you expect a struggle as he will want to stay and be part of the Games. *How will you approach this?*

3. Your entire squad are attending a social function at the British Embassy. You notice that one of your athletes is drinking too much at this event, and this is strangely out of character for her. *What needs to be done – if anything?*

4. You are on a bus going to the competition venue and the traffic problems are diabolical. Traffic has been bad throughout the Games, but this is much worse than normal. Some athletes begin to pester you. They are frightened that they will miss the match/heat/bout. *What will you do about this?*

5. You get a message from one of your athletes that another member of your squad has been arrested by police in the downtown area. He's been accused of shop-lifting. *How should you handle this?*

6. A worried athlete confides in you and says that the team physiotherapist is undermining the coach when she is talking to the athletes during treatment sessions. *Any thoughts on what to do here?*

In both the managers' and the netballers' sessions at least one of the aims was to develop a closer team of people who would have had a shared experience and, it may be hoped, some amusement during those sessions.

However, another goal was to give them some clues as to how they might think about reacting when and if they were faced with similar situations.

Benchmarking in Sport

Ultimately, competing in sport is a benchmarking activity. Quite simply you measure yourself against other teams or competitors. The coaching staff for the 1996 British rowing team were interested in measuring themselves against the benchmark of other coaching groups around the world. In the end, it would be rower competing against rower rather than coach versus coach, but the thought processes were nevertheless interesting. If we were making improvements on an annual basis – but those teams who were ahead of us were also making similar improvements – then we would never overtake them. It was as if all the teams from around the world were improving; but, in fact the gaps were not being closed and hence the status quo remained.

The coaches started a programme of self-improvement in 1995 with a view to raising their own standard. It was to be as if the coaches would actually be competing against the foreign coaches. They wanted to close the gap on some of the other nations by doing something a little more radical. Self-improvement was seen as such an approach to this problem. They went through many team-building exercises of a similar nature to those already mentioned in this chapter.

A slightly different version dealt with the coaches' identifying what *they* saw as the critical success factors for an elite rower. What were the key attributes exhibited by some of the best British oarsmen and women, as well as their foreign counterparts? After much discussion and finally a vote on the matter the attributes identified by some of Britain's best rowing coaches were, in rank order:

- high levels of intrinsic motivation
- good sense of self-belief
- calmness under pressure
- natural competitiveness
- copes well with pressure
- never gives up
- seeks perfection

Having agreed that this was the 'perfect profile', we then set about working with the existing squad to look for ways of improving them against this model. The exercise had helped in two ways: it was a team-building exercise among the staff, and it also showed the athletes that the staff were prepared to do something about their own performance as the Games approached. The coaching 'team' would have to work together under extreme pressure in the following 18 months and they were well aware that they would improve their chances of success if they were a more cohesive unit.

Summary

The issue of team building and cohesiveness is not straightforward. I have been exposed to some very talented groups who had poor off-field cohesiveness and yet were successful on the field of play. Equally I have seen some underperforming groups who had little cohesiveness on and off the field. There are no hard and fast rules, but my general approach is based around the idea that if the coach and/or the management are interested in enhancing team cohesion then I will employ an array of techniques to improve this situation. If asked for my opinion, I will tend to encourage this approach because I feel that improved cohesiveness rarely reduces performance and may certainly make the total sporting experience far more enjoyable for those involved.

CHAPTER NINE

Dealing with Injury

When I injured my shoulder I couldn't do anything. No work-outs, nothing. I was angry, moody, frustrated and I realized then just how much tennis meant to me. It's my life.

Steffi Graf, world-class tennis player

This year I have hardly stepped on the track. I have not run for the last five weeks and am still pessimistic. All my traditional doubts are reappearing. I am twenty-six years old with virtually no work experience. What can I do in the future? What happens if I never run successfully again? I imagine the next few years disappearing in a sequence of frustrating problems, culminating in unemployment as a disillusioned, bitter ex-athlete. As a full-time athlete, injury becomes all the more frustrating because his or her livelihood is threatened.

Jack Buckner, world-class distance runner

An injury to an elite sportsman or woman may elicit strong emotional reactions. These come to the fore when a usually active person is forced to endure extended periods of inactivity and deal with the uncertainty surrounding his prospects within his chosen sport. Sports medicine doctors primarily concern themselves with the physical aspects of injury rehabilitation, and, unfortunately, this has led to instances where it is assumed that because the body has healed the mind must be fine as well. Clearly this is not always the case. Some athletes psychologically adjust to injury quite readily, but for others the process is complicated.

According to sports medicine experts, the number of injuries occurring in most sports is increasing. It seems that while technological advances may help to improve certain safety aspects in sport, this fails to compensate for the increased training load that athletes endure in pursuit of improved performances. The incidence of injury is high with eight out of ten being injured in a career lasting more than five years. Sport is a breeding ground for injury.

In the last fifteen years much has been written about the psychology of injury. Before this there was a tendency to dwell on an injury's physical aspects. Medical experts, more often than not, attended only to the physical consequences of injury.

Sports medicine has made great advances in the physical rehabilitation of injured athletes, but until the late 1980s little attention had been given to their psychological rehabilitation. This chapter presents details from some of the recent literature and suggests strategies for helping elite athletes back to competition. It also includes a discussion concerning the psychological predictors of injury as well as issues relating to athletes' adhering to rehabilitation programmes.

Certainly some athletes psychologically adapt to injury quite readily, but unfortunately many more do not. It is important to help athletes understand that injury management is a skill, and, just like their other sports skills, it is something that requires commitment and sustained effort. Athletes should be encouraged to acquire the skill of injury rehabilitation. It is not enough for them to recover physically; they must also recover mentally and emotionally and often this needs to occur first.

Olympic champion hockey player Sean Kerly is treated pitch-side for an injury.

Reacting to Injury

Some authors have described the response of athletes to injury as a grief reaction. The extent of the psychological injury obviously varies greatly with athletes' personal attributes. For example, their psychological characteristics vary in such areas as level of self-esteem, anxiety and intrinsic motivation. All of these factors are likely to affect an athlete's response to injury and rehabilitation. The American researcher Bob Rotella (1982) believes that a serious injury which sidelines an elite athlete may be almost as devastating as the loss of a loved one. He likens it to a bereavement. For some athletes their entire sense of well-being is tied up with their sporting prowess and if this is taken away from them, even temporarily, it may be viewed as a significant loss.

Sport psychologists working with an injured athlete often see the five stages of adaptation that Kubler-Ross listed in her classic work *On Death and Dying* (1969): denial, anger, bargaining, depression and acceptance. **Figure 21** shows some hypothetical athlete reactions during each of the stages.

Denial 'I'll be OK.'; 'It isn't that bad.'
Anger 'Why did that clown pass to me!'; 'What was that ref doing?'
Bargaining 'OK, it's bad, but let me play today and I'll get treatment after the match.'
Depression 'This is hopeless – I'll never get back.'; 'I'm still not better even after two weeks' treatment.'
Acceptance 'OK, I've now got to get on with it and make sure I act like a professional athlete. It's no good complaining, I've just got to attend physiotherapy every day.'

Fig 21

Other workers in the area have suggested that this bereavement response goes through three phases. The first is characterized by a sudden shock-like state, an immediate response to injury. Common emotions during this time are anger, denial of the injury and bargaining behaviours. The second phase involves intense preoccupation with the injury; during this time athletes may experience insomnia, fatigue, crying or troubling dreams. Depression is a common emotional reaction for athletes in this phase. The last phase is based on reorganization. This is where the athletes begin to display renewed interest and return to previously important activities, including their sport. Acceptance of the situation is the key to this stage of injury-related grief.

The denial and bargaining behaviours may interfere with rehabilitation. Anger and depression are more understandable states, but they may still hinder recovery. The health professionals should be concerned with speeding up the transition from denial to acceptance. I have found that the art of WID may be of use in this area. WID stands for 'winning inner dialogue' and refers to a cognitive approach to injury rehabilitation. The concept was introduced for patients coping with the trauma of disease-related surgery in general medicine. Sport psychologists have modified the technique in such a way that it has become a specific psychological rehabilitation strategy that can be taught. By comparison, DID ('defeating inner dialogue') represents a different, more negative perspective. WID is based around the inner conversation that we all use from time to time. We often talk ourselves into or out of things. Somebody says, 'Oh, I'm a terrible cook – I can't even boil an egg properly.' Or another says, 'I always get a cold when winter comes.' These are both fairly trivial examples of our own inner dialogues, but you can guess the consequences of these repeated statements.

Let us look at a more pertinent sporting example. The physiotherapist does not turn up at the sports centre when the athlete has booked in for another appointment. An athlete who is using DID will probably get frustrated by this and adopt the attitude that, 'That's all I need. I can't even get treatment for my injury. Right, well I'm off then – I'm not going to waste my time here. What's the point?' As a result the athlete will probably miss a treatment session, he will become tense and agitated and simply make matters worse. However, an athlete using WID is more likely to wait around longer if the physiotherapist does not turn up. He is more likely to organize another session as soon as possible and to go off and do some of the rehabilitation exercises (specific stretches for a hamstring injury, for example).

So while the DID athlete has probably gone away muttering to himself and eating a bar of chocolate, the WID athlete is getting on with the business of rehabilitation. The non-arrival of a physiotherapist is a trivial example but it is an illustration of something that I have witnessed on several occasions. The truly successful athletes will be using WID to get on with whatever is possible. Others will simply use DID to make life harder for themselves.

Injured athletes who are having to be uncharacteristically inactive, are prone to using DID. This is where the sport psychologist can pre-empt further problems that are likely to occur which might slow down the movement from denial to acceptance. The consequences of the WID strategy are positive, while the DID causes problems.

WID can be used in conjunction with a technique known as 'thought stopping'. Injured athletes are sensitized to their inner dialogues from the outset. By repeating the word 'stop' whenever DID comments come to mind the athlete may effectively turn self-defeating anxiety into more positive reflection.

It is important to let the athlete know that it is perfectly normal to go through such phases and he should not regard himself as 'weak' or 'weird' to experience such thoughts. Athletes within the AIMS programme discuss injury and illness when they are fit. In this way they are better prepared for the almost inevitable injury when it does occur.

Research suggests that there are certain critical punctuation marks in the response to severe injury and these give us a clue as to when a psychological input might be appropriate. The first 24 hours are fairly critical. This is where the anger and mood swings are likely to show up. Interestingly, the five to seven-days period is also seen as important. At this time the athlete is likely to be obsessive about his condition and one respected author in this field even warns against suicidal tendencies for certain individuals. And, finally, the 28-day mark also seems to be important. This is when athletes are ready to fully adjust to their condition and can begin to see a light at the end of the tunnel.

Clearly the severity of the injury, the athlete's personality, age and experience will all have an influence on the significance and timing of these periods, but the rule of 'one day, one week and one month' being critical is a useful starting point.

If we accept that athletes will typically go through the phases mentioned above, it is not surprising that their self-confidence may be affected. If they have been used to seeing their coach three or four times a week, or hearing from their team-mates on a regular basis and suddenly this no longer happens, then it is not surprising that the emotional responses might be greater and that psychological rehabilitation may take longer.

Recovering from Injury

During the period of recovery the athlete should be encouraged to use goal-setting as a means of planning for the future and a return to sport. One athlete currently confined to an exercise bicycle is gradually clocking up enough imaginary miles to go from John O'Groats to Land's End. He uses a large map pinned up in his bedroom to plot his progress.

In most instances there will be physical activities which can be worked on during this period. The athlete with a knee reconstruction may be working hard on trunk strength perhaps, or increasing the range of movement in the shoulders. I have known athletes who have turned their temporary incapacitation into an opportunity to work on some weakness in their armoury. Remedial flexibility work is a favourite with many elite performers and several athletes have enhanced their hand–eye co-ordination by learning to juggle while injured. Athletes should be encouraged to set goals for themselves, particularly if the injury is so debilitating that they cannot swim or cycle.

The second important element of the rehabilitation programme is to find out what exercise can be performed without hindering the recovery process. With most common athletic injuries there is something physical that can be done. An injured thrower I worked with once took the opportunity to develop a rigorous flexibility regime. He had been a noted 'Mr Plank' with little range of movement in the lower back and upper body. During his two-month lay-off he made great progress in this area and returned to throwing as a more dynamic athlete because of this commitment.

Athletes with leg injuries can often cope with swimming pool work. Flotation jackets can be used to allow athletes to go through leg exercises without having to support their own bodyweight. It is vital that the athlete asks the doctor what is permissible. It is not just a matter of finding out, 'When can I compete or train again?' The athlete should get specific guidance on what is and is not advisable. Often the doctor will recommend that the athlete should see a physiotherapist and he should be able to give the athlete some supplementary exercises that can be

Olympic sculler Silken Lauman, complete with medal and walking stick.

performed. But knowing which exercises to do is not enough. The athlete will then have to make the commitment to work at them, even when there appears to be no progress being made.

At the same time the athlete can be improving his tactical/technical appreciation of his sport. He can be guided towards books, magazines and videotape footage which will assist him in his learning and help him to maintain his competency.

The athletes can also be given guidance concerning nutritional control during this phase. Presumably they will not be expending as much energy as when they were in full training and thus they may need advice on how to slightly reduce or modify their intake.

Finally, some elite athletes have used this period of relative inactivity to learn various mental techniques which will help them to return to competition and be better able to control such variables as concentration, motivation and activation. For example, they can learn the techniques of relaxation, visualization, self-talk and self-regulation.

I have found that the Sports Priming Process (SPP) can be an effective mental technique in this regard. Athletes have been encouraged to experiment with a variety of creative images to help them to supplement the healing process. Many of these ideas have been adapted from the work of the Canadian sport psychologist Terry Orlick.

Healing images

Treatment modalities	Ultrasound as creating a healing glow Therapeutic application of ice as freezing up and shutting down pain receptors Laser treatment eating away the damaged tissues
Rehabilitation activity	Blood surging to the muscle and rebuilding it at an accelerated rate during resistance training Muscles growing as mobility exercises completed
Medication	Non-steroidal anti-inflammatory medication as sponges absorbing local tissue irritants Pain-killing injections burning off the damaged tissues
Mental training	Deep breathing as infusing the body with a healing energy Concentration drills as opening gates that release endorphins into the circulation

Fig 22

Healed images

Shoulder injury	Ligaments as a combination of wound steel and rubber, strong but flexible
Knee injury	The meniscus as smooth as silk following surgery
Foot injury	The bone structure as internally buttressed by a new network of bone, strong yet yielding like a suspension bridge (following stress fracture)
Back injury	The spinal column supported by tendon, ligament and muscle like the rigging of a sailing ship
Fracture healing	The bone is protected by an outer sheath of flexible metal

Fig 23

Predisposition towards Injury

While working at the Australian Institute of Sport in Canberra, I was involved in research with the sports medicine team which analysed the relationship between personality variables and injury rates for one year. Among many findings we discovered that there were some personality factors which could be used to predict injuries; but in most cases there was little correlation between personality and injury rates. By itself, it is doubtful whether a personality test could be used to predict injuries, but, when used in tandem with other measures, it is useful. For instance, life stress and stressors have been consistently reported as contributing to both illness and injury.

Research suggests that if an athlete experiences one or more of life's major stressors such as bereavement, separation/divorce, loss of job, important examinations or moving house he or she is more vulnerable to injury and illness. It has been suggested that such events hinder concentration and distract the athlete from vital cues. The athlete fails to notice something important (such as a pot-hole in the road while out running) and sustains an injury. It has also been suggested that these life stressors exhaust the athlete's energy resources and that he or she takes a 'tired body' to the training session. This tiredness in turn means that the athlete will, in effect, undergo a tougher workload. This then has a knock-on effect because the athlete takes an even more fatigued body to the next training session. Over a period of time this cumulative effect will put the athlete at risk, particularly if there is also the typical problem of poor sleep patterns.

Sport psychology researchers are also starting to look at minor, day-to-day stressors. It is fairly well agreed that major events such as bereavement and divorce are traumatic and stressful. But in some respects perhaps it is the minor but more frequent stressors that take their toll. These could include such things as arduous daily commuting or pressures at work or constant financial problems. I suspect that we need to know a lot more about this aspect of stress before we shall be able to make major improvements in this field. While it is obvious that some injuries occur through bad luck or unforeseen circumstances, there is no doubt that an analysis of life stress could help to reduce the risk of injury. Training to the limit will always be something of a gamble, but with some thought and planning it is possible to change the odds in the athlete's favour.

Dispositional optimism is a general expectancy for good rather than bad things to occur. Such general expectancies are believed to influence health because they determine the extent to which an individual is willing to initiate health-oriented behaviour and persist with them in the face of difficulties. Links have been found between dispositional optimism and health in such conditions as recovery from coronary artery bypass surgery. Researchers assessed mood and coping strategies before surgery, physiological reactions during surgery and progress after surgery among 'optimists' and 'pessimists'.

Optimists reported less hostility and depression than did pessimists immediately before surgery. They also made plans and set goals for recovery before the operation to a greater extent than did pessimists. Measures taken during surgery showed fewer adverse physiological reactions for the optimists. Also the optimists recovered faster in terms of objective recovery milestones and in terms of subjective ratings of improvement by members of the rehabilitation team.

It has been suggested that both behavioural and physiological mechanisms could be responsible for the optimism–health connection. Optimists show a tendency to accept the reality of negative situations; engage in direct, problem-focused coping; use positive reinterpretations and seek social support. They are also less likely to become preoccupied with their emotional distress.

Social Support for the Injured Athlete

After stressful events people turn to those closest to them as a source of strength. It is those closest to us who carry our burdens when we are incapable; who offer a shoulder on which to cry, shelter from adversity and solace from grief. Significant others share their resources to help those for whom they care through these most difficult periods of life.

(Hobfoll and Stephens, 1990)

Research into those athletes who stick with their injury rehabilitation programmes reveals one common factor – they receive good social support from others when compared with those athletes who do not adhere as well. These significant others could be coaches, husbands, friends, physiotherapists or whoever, but if they show a genuine interest in the recovery process then the chances of adherence are greatly increased. It helps if you can be a good listener and have empathy with the athlete.

The stress of injury may act as a threat to an athlete's identity, self-concept, belief system, social and occupational functioning, and emotional equilibrium. Injury may force athletes to:

- accept a new definition of their abilities
- redefine their role on the team
- change their current level of involvement
- redirect future career opportunities.

Against this backdrop it could be argued that social support is the key in the injury rehabilitation process. Research has demonstrated that support provided by others is helpful in coping with life stress, crisis, mental and physical illness, unemployment, job stress and bereavement. Supported individuals are generally more mentally and physically healthy than unsupported ones, perhaps due to the health-sustaining and stress-reducing functions of social support.

Social support is a multi-dimensional construct. It is a form of social commerce. It represents an exchange of resources between at least two people, with the outcome being the enhancement of the recipients' well-being.

The Dimensions of Social Support

Listening support	Behaviours that indicate that people listen to you without being judgemental
Emotional support	Behaviours that comfort you and indicate that people are on your side
Emotional challenge	Behaviours that challenge you to evaluate your attitudes, values and feelings
Task appreciation	Behaviours that acknowledge your efforts and express appreciation for the work you do
Task challenge	Behaviours that challenge your way of thinking about your work in order to stretch and motivate you and lead you to greater creativity
Reality confirmation	Behaviours that indicate that people are similar to you – see things the way you do
Material assistance	Behaviours that provide you with money, products and gifts
Personal assistance	Behaviours that indicate a giving of time, skills, knowledge, and/or expertise to help you accomplish your tasks

Fig 24

A team of people offering social support to the rehabilitating athlete would do well to provide all the dimensions of social support listed above. While it is the medical team which will concentrate on the physical aspects of rehabilitation, it is often the unofficial 'team' of friends and family who will be best placed to offer the appropriate social support. Both teams have a role to play in returning the athlete to competition.

Injuries in sport are virtually inevitable. Therefore it is vital that athletes and coaches prepare for them in advance. They need to have a strategy in place before injury strikes and they need to invest time and effort in the fine tuning of this strategy. Athletes should accept the challenge that injury rehabilitation is as important as any of the other sports skills they need to acquire.

CHAPTER TEN

Retiring from Sport

It is 19 years since I was competing... a long time since the end of my swimming career, a long transition during which I was so confused and bewildered by my range of emotions in relation to my career and its ending. I am getting to the coping stage only by becoming informed and educating myself about the normal athletic retirement process.

Shane Gould, winner of five Olympic swimming medals
at the age of 15, talking in 1992

There was a feeling of loss – of being made redundant – because the sport had no real need for me. I couldn't understand that having devoted my entire life to the sport I was left sitting on the bench with nothing to do.

Fatima Whitbread, former world champion javelin thrower

Life is made up of a number of transitions. Transitional events are inevitable and include leaving the parental home, going away to university, getting married, having children and career changes. Every transition is different and each has the potential to be either positive or negative and all variants in between. Any transition requires a degree of adjustment, and most individuals can cope with several during a lifetime.

It is apparent that many former athletes have difficulties during the transition process which sees them leaving their sporting careers. Their transitions are often happening at a relatively early age and some are not well-equipped to cope with the process. Unfortunately, some of the skill sets required for their new non-sporting career are often different from those utilized when they were still competing. They may also have unresolved emotions and feelings, and in some cases this has led to potential health problems for those individuals. Research conducted in the 1980s certainly suggested that two out of every three elite, retiring athletes had adjustment problems when they left their sport (Orlick and Werthner, 1987).

However, it also has to be acknowledged that for some athletes, retiring from high-level sport is like a form of release – an escape. When talking to a group of British rowers before they left for the 1996 Atlanta Olympics, I was struck that those athletes in their late twenties or older were really quite keen to get the entire thing finished so that they could 'get on with a normal life'. Of course, these comments might have been a reflection of the tough training programme which they were currently enduring, and they also had yet to experience life after competition so that they had nothing with which to compare it. Nevertheless, retirement from sport was certainly being eagerly anticipated because it would allow for new opportunities for personal growth and development.

When talking to competitors who have retired from top level sport one meets two types of response, with various 'shades' in between. There are those athletes who see retiring as a form of dying, and there are those who regard it as a rebirth. Clearly, where possible we should be favouring the latter response, and coaches, administrators, team doctors and psychologists should be endeavouring to create an environment in which this can happen.

Athletes who have difficulty in making the transition often talk about problems relating to their loss of status, not having the skill sets required for success in the 'working' world, and missing out on the social side of their sport once they leave it. Those athletes who eventually work their way through these problems will often talk about the techniques they employed to survive this adjustment process. These may include switching to another focus of interest, maintaining a certain level of physical conditioning by doing some form of sports training, and generally keeping busy.

In my experience, those athletes who adjust to retirement fairly easily are those who had planned ahead and knew that they had some other interests to which they could switch their attention. Perhaps it was a field of study that had been neglected while they pursued their sporting goals, or another sport which had been considered too dangerous while they were still competing. There are several competitors on the AIMS programme who have had a longing to do things such as skiing, climbing or parachuting, but their coaches have always been disinclined to arrange for such distractions!

It also seems to be that those athletes who are successful in sport and who can say that they achieved their goals in major competitions also seem to have somewhat smoother transitions. There are some exceptions to this rule, of course, but it holds true for many.

It has to be remembered that retirement from sport is not always an active decision made by the competitor. Those athletes who know for a fact that they will retire at the end of the season in which they have competed at their fifth world championships and their second Olympic Games, or when they have received their hundredth cap would certainly seem to have been able to plan or control the process to a degree. Some of the major difficulties arise when the athlete has little or no say in the timing of retirement, for instance, when an injury occurs or when a coach makes a decision which in effect retires the athlete from international competition. Some of these individuals have a hard time in coming to terms with the transition process because it was mandated rather than voluntary.

There is also a group of athletes who feel ignored or forgotten by their sports colleagues when they retire. Elite performers from so-called amateur Olympic sports will often talk about a sense of feeling as if they were mere commodities which were used by their national governing bodies. When they were past their 'shelf life' they were dropped or discarded. These athletes often find themselves cut off from whatever modest source of funding they once had, and often excluded from the medical insurance scheme they enjoyed while they were seen as being useful to the sport. They also feel that more should be done in terms of education and preparation for the issues which will face them when they retire.

Another issue relates to the timing of advice concerning the retirement process. Some coaches have suggested that even to broach the topic of retirement during the active career of an athlete is likely to distract from competitive performance. They would argue that by planting the seeds of doubt in the athletes' minds they would be doing them a disservice. The contrary argument suggests that by talking openly about some of the likely pitfalls of retirement the athletes can at least feel reassured that their club or organization is taking care of them or looking after their wider interests. In other words, the anxiety levels are reduced because a source of stress is reduced or eliminated.

During the last decade I have offered some support to athletes who have retired from competitive sport, and the remaining part of this chapter will focus on the advice given. In many instances it was given in the weeks or months following an Olympic Games, but in several cases the discussions took place at training camps months in advance of the Games, and on a few occasions it actually took place within the confines of the Olympic village.

Most of the pre-retirement counselling sessions took place on an individual basis. The meetings were designed to raise issues for the competitors and invariably they meant that athletes would go away, do some homework and then return for another discussion. Thankfully, many of the athletes had been trained by coaches who worked on the theme of empowerment. The coaches had encouraged the competitors to demonstrate initiative during their careers, so that they were never entirely dependent upon the coaches. Hence, asking these athletes to think and plan for themselves was not asking for anything unusual.

However, there are some athletes who have not been as lucky. The predominant coaching style in their careers has been one of disempowerment and any athletes in this environment are likely to have little independence and hence the wrench when they leave sport is likely to be far greater. Furthermore, in these circumstances, the athlete is less likely to be effective as an organizer and planner.

During the pre-retirement counselling sessions I was always interested in examining the several social elements within the athlete's life. On the one hand I wanted to know about the level of social support that was likely to be available after retirement, and on the other I wanted to judge the level of social skills already possessed by the athlete.

Experience has shown that athletes who have little or no social support available to them are likely to have a more difficult transition when they leave sport. If their main social circle was formed around their sporting involvement and this then disappears and is not readily replaced by another, it is almost inevitable that problems will occur. One important component in the transition process is the ability to be able to talk about any problems or unresolved issues. Clearly, it helps if there are family, friends or colleagues with whom to talk things through. Hence, if it becomes apparent that an athlete has little social support available before or during the retirement process this starts alarm bells ringing for me.

With regard to social skills, the bells also start ringing if it is apparent that the retiring performer does not have some of the sensitivities normally associated with people in their late twenties or thirties. It has to be said that many elite performers have led a somewhat indulged or cosseted lifestyle in consequence of their sporting prowess. They were often the best athletes at school or in their families. People around them have made allowances for them since they were quite young. Others have made a fuss of them and flattered them on a regular basis. Indeed, people involved in sport have deliberately set out to give these athletes a high sense of self-worth. As a consequence, some of them are self-confident to the point of arrogance and this is an attribute which is not necessarily guaranteed to win friends and influence people away from the sporting world. Accordingly, some elite athletes lack the necessary social skills needed when a new social situation requires sensitivity and tact.

A combination of a minimal level of social support and inappropriate social skills may cause significant problems in the transition process. My job is to make retiring athletes aware of these issues if they exist in their circumstances and then work towards improving the situation. Typically this involves work on goal-setting and the examining of behavioural strategies for increasing their circle of friends and skills away from sport.

There are other warning signals which may emerge from any pre-retirement counselling session. These could include the athlete's identifying too strongly with the sport, or the existence of a significant gap between the athlete's aspirations and ability, or the athlete's having a history of emotional outbursts while competing in sport. There is no research evidence to link these factors with difficulties in the transition process, but anecdotally there seems to be a connection.

If an athlete views himself as 'only' a hockey player or a rower then this may certainly cause problems. The reality is that we are normally more than this. We are each a son or a daughter, a student, a worker, a partner, a loved one, a sports fan or whatever. But we are seldom 'just' an athlete. Yet I have known many elite athletes who are prone to discounting the value of anything else they have in their lives, including relationships and parallel careers. Perhaps they believed that the only way to reach the top was to be focused and single-minded and they did not want to be seen to be having any distractions in their lives. This is an erroneous perception on their part, but it might as well be true if they believe it to be so. Athletes who adopt this extreme viewpoint are more likely to be at risk during the transition process.

Athletes who are extremely motivated but who perhaps do not possess the ability to be of truly world class may also be candidates for problems during the retirement transition. They may often and almost inevitably reach the end of their careers having failed to achieve their ultimate goals. There may be a sense of having 'unfinished business' once they retire. Objective observers might conclude that they had done well to represent their country, but the athlete aspired to standing on the Olympic medal rostrum. There is clearly a mismatch and sadly some of the worst cases of maladjustment have been with ex-athletes who had little or no chance of achieving the goals they had set themselves.

Athletes who have difficulty controlling their emotions at times of great pressure also tend to have more problems when making the transition towards retirement. All athletes respond in some way to competitive pressure, but those who typically lose control or who lose their sense of proportion are most at risk. It is one thing for someone like John McEnroe to 'manipulate' an emotional reaction, but it is another for someone who does not intend these outbursts to happen.

So if it is acknowledged that certain types of athlete are likely to have difficulties when it comes to retirement, what can the AIMS programme do to help? Quite simply, it is all about the transfer of skills and attributes mentioned in all the earlier chapters. It is about teaching the athletes that they have certain insights, experiences or outlooks which can be welcomed and desired by potential employers and friends. It is also about informing athletes that they may have certain gaps or limitations in their personal make-up and that they need to work on these. They need to set goals, they need to work on processes to achieve outcomes, and they need to focus on controlling the controllables. They must focus on the correct and important elements of performing in their new environments.

The athletes are taught that their new careers also require the use of mental skills. When applying for jobs or trying to impress people they can say, with some conviction, that through sport they have learned to perform well when under pressure, they know how to communicate well, they are highly goal-oriented, they can handle and learn from criticism, they have typically travelled around the world and dealt with different cultures, they know about adhering to tough programmes, they can stay focused and single-minded, and they have developed a range of mental skills to allow them to achieve their full potential. These attributes are welcomed and cherished in many walks of life and athletes need to be convinced accordingly.

Self-Regulation Techniques in Sport

In modern society there is a growing interest in non-pharmacological, self-induced, altered states of consciousness because of their suggested benefits for better mental and physical health. Western interest in relaxation techniques in particular may be traced back at least to the time before the Second World War, but the yogis of India were certainly pioneering the field more than two thousand years ago. This appendix focuses on the ways in which athletes are being encouraged to experiment with such techniques in order to improve their performances when competing in pressurized situations.

The major benefits of relaxation training for athletes are:

- relaxation prepares them for mental imagery
- relaxation improves concentration ability
- relaxation helps them to control arousal levels
- relaxation helps them to sleep better
- relaxation helps to improve body awareness
- relaxation reduces recovery time.

Two specific techniques were developed for athletes involved in the AIMS programme: Modal Ten Relaxation (MTR) and Clock Relaxation (CR) were developed in an attempt to reduce the physical symptoms associated with increased tension in the days leading to a competition. These techniques have been used by Australian, New Zealand and British international athletes from such sports as track and field, rugby league, hockey, rowing, judo and netball. The techniques are schematically represented in **Figures 25 and 26**.

One traditional technique employed by psychologists to reduce somatic or physical stress is Progressive Muscle Relaxation (PMR). This technique involves the successive tensing and relaxing of major muscle groups. However, several experienced athletes had complained that they found the maximal contractions in PMR too sapping in the days leading up to major competitions. On a psychological level they preferred to wait for the competition day before going for any maximum efforts. It was almost as if they did not want to burn up their strength reserves in those vital last days. It was obvious that alternatives would have to be

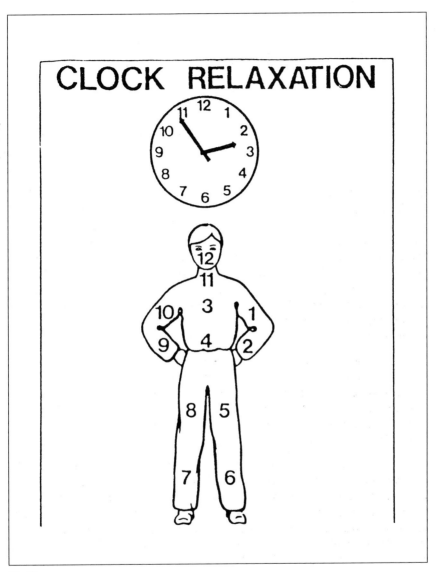

Fig 25

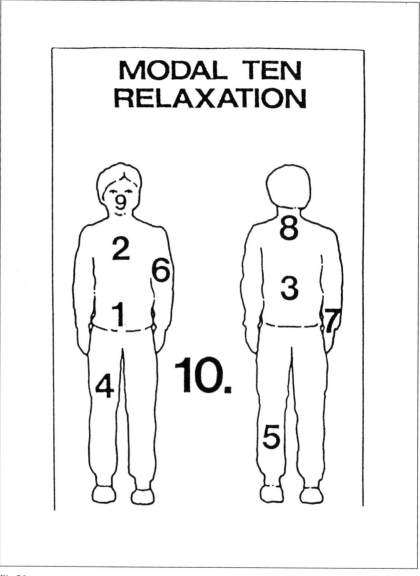

Fig 26

developed because, despite some of the athletes' reservations about PMR, the unwanted stress symptom of increased muscular tension was still present as they prepared for competition.

Some athletes experience a marked elevation in residual levels of tension that increases the probability of injury and subsequent under-achievement in performance. While PMR remains a useful relaxation technique in some circumstances, it is not as appropriate immediately before the competition season. MTR and CR are the results of experiments with a variety of relaxation techniques that have previously been recommended by leaders in the field. They are hybrid versions that have been developed specifically for sportsmen and women.

The two techniques include the same passive focus on successive muscle groups, but the sequence is different. MTR was the first to be developed and CR followed when it became obvious that regular users became slightly bored with the same sequence over and over again. However, both techniques are based on the same principle – that the athletes should focus on assessing the amount of relaxation present in a variety of muscle groups. They are asked to experience the sensation passively rather than by trying to modify the level by any physical movement. Adopting a comfortable position (sitting or lying) with eyes closed, the athlete focuses on each muscle group for approximately 30 to 60 seconds. The sequence of muscle groups for each technique are listed below. The athlete is then asked to assess the level of relaxation in each muscle – almost as if he were using a rating scale of 1 to 10.

Modal Ten Relaxation

1. Stomach
2. Chest
3. Lower back
4. Thighs
5. Calves
6. Biceps
7. Forearms
8. Shoulders
9. Face and jaw
10. Entire body

Clock Relaxation

1. Left bicep
2. Left forearm
3. Chest
4. Stomach
5. Left thigh
6. Left calf
7. Right calf
8. Right thigh
9. Right forearm
10. Right bicep
11. Shoulders
12. Face and jaw

Most athletes are 'in tune' with their physical responses and find this task relatively simple to complete. Depending upon his current fitness status or the nature of his most recent training session, the athlete will have a range of sensations across the major muscles. Some muscles will probably feel quite tired or even sore. This does not matter. Experience has shown that if the athlete can concentrate exclusively on the muscle group in question the relaxation response will follow automatically.

MTR takes about 12 minutes to complete and CR takes just a little longer. Athletes are able to learn the technique and to practise by themselves. I have used one or both of these techniques with athletes in the Commonwealth Games of 1986 and 1990, and the 1988, 1992 and 1996 Olympics.

The remainder of this appendix focuses on some of the more common and standard examples of self-regulation techniques. They are included here because they may be safely practised without supervision. There is no one technique that is better than any other. I have found that different athletes respond well to different skills, in no very predictable manner. I advise AIMS' athletes to learn at least two techniques from each of the sections. I have gradually modified the techniques as I have worked with a variety of athletes. I do not believe in assigning any contemporary authors' names to the techniques as I am sure that similar techniques have been in use for many years.

I have accumulated the current list of techniques for the AIMS programme by attending seminars and courses in several parts of the world and each skill outlined here has been modified in some way because of my contact with gifted athletes, who typically live with a heightened level of bodily awareness. They seem able to bypass some of the rudimentary steps. The techniques explained in the remainder of the appendix are:

Somatic relaxation techniques

progressive muscle relaxation
local progressive relaxation
localized relaxation
local loosening
descent relaxation
systematic loosening
modal ten relaxation

Breathing control techniques

alpha breathing
quiet breathing
centering
pendulum breathing
modal ten breathing

Somatic Relaxation Techniques

Progressive Muscle Relaxation (PMR)

Settle back as comfortably as you can, with your eyes closed. Let yourself relax to the best of your ability. Now, as you relax, clench your right fist; clench it tighter and tighter, and study the tension as you do so.

Keep it clenched and feel the tension in your right fist, hand, forearm – and now relax. Let the fingers of your right hand become loose, and observe the contrast in your feelings. Once more, clench your right fist really tight – hold it, and notice the tension again… now let go, and relax. Let your fingers straighten out and notice the difference once more.

Now repeat that with your left fist. Clench your left fist while the rest of your body relaxes; clench that fist tighter and feel the tension… and now relax. Again enjoy the contrast. Repeat that once more, clench the left fist, tight and tense. Now do the opposite of tension – relax and feel the difference. Continue relaxing like that for a while. Clench both fists tighter and tighter, both fists tense, forearms tense, study the sensations… and relax; straighten out your fingers and feel that relaxation. Continue relaxing your hands and forearms more and more. Now bend your elbows and tense your biceps, tense them harder and harder and study the tension feelings… then, straighten out your arms, let them relax and feel that difference again. Let the relaxation develop.

Once more, tense your biceps; hold the tension and observe it carefully. Straighten the arms and relax; relax to the best of your ability. Each time, give close attention to your feelings when you tense up and when you relax. Now straighten your arms so that you feel most tension in the triceps muscles along the back of your arms; stretch your arms and feel that tension… and now relax. Get your arms back into a comfortable position. Let the relaxation proceed on its own. The arms should feel comfortably heavy as you allow them to relax. Straighten the arms once more so that you feel the tension in the triceps muscles – straighten them. Feel that tension… and relax.

Now let's concentrate on pure relaxation in the arms without any tension. Get your arms comfortable and let them relax further and further. Continue relaxing your arms even further. Even when your arms seem fully relaxed try to go that extra bit further; try to achieve deeper and deeper levels of relaxation.

Crinkle up your forehead now; wrinkle it tighter. And now stop wrinkling your forehead, relax and smooth it out. Picture the entire forehead and scalp becoming smoother as the relaxation increases. Now frown and crease your brows and study the tension. Let go of the tension again. Smooth out the forehead once more. Now clench your jaws, bite your teeth together; study the tension throughout the jaws… relax your jaws now. Let your lips part slightly. Appreciate the relaxation. Now press your tongue hard against the roof of your mouth. Look for the tension... now let your tongue return to a comfortable and relaxed position.

Now purse your lips, press your lips together tighter and tighter... relax the lips. Note the contrast between tension and relaxation. Feel the relaxation all over your face, all over your forehead and scalp, eyes, jaws, lips, tongue and throat. The relaxation progresses further and further.

Now attend to your neck muscles. Press your head back as far as it can go and feel the tension in the neck; roll your head to the right and feel the tension shift; now roll it to the left. Straighten your head and bring it forward, press your chin against your chest. Let your head return to a comfortable position, and study the relaxation. Let the relaxation develop. Shrug your shoulders, right up. Hold the tension... Drop your shoulders and feel the relaxation. Neck and shoulders relaxed. Shrug your shoulders again and move them around. Bring your shoulders up and forward and back. Feel the tension in your shoulders and in your upper back... Drop your shoulders once more and relax. Let the relaxation spread down into the shoulders, right into your back muscles; relax your neck and throat, and your jaws and other facial areas as the pure relaxation takes over and grows deeper and deeper and deeper.

Breathe easily and freely in and out. Notice how the relaxation increases as you exhale – as you breathe out just feel the relaxation. Now breathe right in and fill your lungs; inhale deeply and hold your breath. Study the tension... Now exhale, let the walls of your chest grow loose and push the air out automatically. Continue relaxing and breathe freely and gently. Feel the relaxation and enjoy it. With the rest of your body as relaxed as possible, fill your lungs again. Breathe in deeply and hold it again. That's fine, breathe out and appreciate the relief. Just breathe normally.

Continue relaxing your chest and let the relaxation spread to your back, shoulders, neck and arms. Merely let go – and enjoy the relaxation. Now let's pay attention to your abdominal muscles, your stomach area. Tighten your stomach muscles, make your abdomen hard. Notice the tension... and relax. Let the muscle loosen and notice the contrast. Once more, press and tighten your stomach muscles. Hold the tension and study it and relax. Notice the general well-being that comes with relaxing your stomach. Now draw your stomach in, pull the muscles right in and feel the tension this way... now relax again. Let your stomach out.

Continue breathing normally and easily and feel the gentle massaging action all over chest and stomach. Now pull your stomach in again and hold the tension. Now push out and tense that; hold the tension. Once more pull in and feel the tension; now relax your stomach fully. Let the tension dissolve as the relaxation grows deeper. Each time you breathe out, notice the rhythmic relaxation both in your lungs and in your stomach. Notice how your chest and stomach relax more and more. Try and let go of all contractions anywhere in your body.

Now direct your attention to your lower back. Arch your back, make your lower back quite hollow, and feel the tension along your spine and settle down comfortably again, relaxing the lower back. Just arch your back and feel the tension as you do so. Try to keep the rest of your body as relaxed as possible. Try to localize the tension throughout your lower back area. Relax once more, relaxing further and further. Relax your lower back, relax your upper back, spread the relaxation to your stomach, chest, shoulders, arms and facial area; these parts relaxing further and further.

Now flex your buttocks and thighs. Flex your thighs by pressing down your heels as hard as you can... relax and note the difference. Straighten your knees and flex your thigh muscles again. Hold the tension... relax your hips and thighs. Allow the relaxation to proceed on its own. Press your feet and toes downwards, away from your face, so that your calf muscles become tense. Study the tension... relax your feet and calves. This time bend your feet towards your face so that you feel tension along your shins. Bring your toes right up... relax again. Keep relaxing for a while.

Now let yourself relax further all over. Relax your feet, ankles, calves and shins, knees, thighs, buttocks and hips. Feel the heaviness of your lower body as you relax still further. Spread the relaxation to your stomach, waist and lower back. Let go more and more. Feel that relaxation all over. Let it proceed to your upper back, chest, shoulders and arms and right to the tips of your fingers. Keep relaxing more and more deeply. Make sure that no tension has crept into your throat; relax your neck and your jaws and all your facial muscles. Keep relaxing your whole body like that for a while.

Let yourself relax.

Local Progressive Relaxation (LPR)

Lie on the floor, with arms by your sides.

Bend the hand of the dominant arm back, fingers straight, as though you are trying to place the back of your hand on your forearm.

Hold that position for approximately 10 seconds, relax and let go.

Identify where the tension is felt. Repeat.

Now bend the hand in such a way that you are trying to touch your fingers to the underside of your forearm. Hold, feel the tension, relax and let go. Repeat.

Repeat the whole sequence with the other arm.

Repeat the sequence with both arms, but generate only half as much tension – relaxing slowly.

Repeat with just enough tension to identify it, hold, relax and let go.

From the forearm muscles move to the dominant upper arm, repeating the sequence, flexing the elbow to put tension in the biceps. Begin with maximum tension, relax, repeat.

Repeat again with half as much tension, relax and repeat.
Repeat with just enough tension to identify, relax, and repeat.
Repeat sequence with non-dominant arm.
Repeat sequence with arms.
Focusing on the extensor muscles of the arm, press down against the floor with both wrists, hold, and relax.
Repeat the sequence by generating only half as much tension and then again with just enough tension to be able to identify it.
Using both arms, slowly increase the tension from fingertips to shoulders without moving. Tighten a little bit more, still more, and continue to gradually increase tension until it is as tense and rigid as you can make it with fists clenched tightly.
Hold, and slowly let the tension go a little bit at a time, a little bit more, continuing until the arms are completely free of tension.
Continue to relax more and more.
Repeat tension and relaxation with only half as much tension and then with just enough to identify the tension.

Localized Relaxation (LR)

Make a tight fist with your left hand. Squeeze it tight. Note how it feels. Now relax.
Once again, squeeze your left hand tightly and study the tension that you feel. And once again, just relax and think of the tension disappearing from your fingers.
Make a tight fist with your right hand. Squeeze it as tight as you can, and note the tension in your fingers and your hand, and your forearm.
Now relax.
Once again, squeeze your right fist tightly.
And again, just relax.
Make a tight fist with your left hand, and bend your arm to make your left biceps hard. Hold it tense. Now relax totally. Feel the warmth escape down your biceps, through your forearm and out of your fingers.
Now make a tight fist with the other hand, and raise your hand to make your right biceps hard. Hold it tight, and feel the tension.
Now relax. Concentrate on the feelings flowing through your arm.
Now squeeze both fists at once and bend both arms to make them totally tense throughout. Hold it, and think about the tension you feel.
Now relax, and feel the total warmth and relaxation flowing through your muscles. All of the tension is flowing out of your fingertips and you will feel quite refreshed.

Local Loosening Drills (LLD)

Kneeling, sitting on a low stool, or standing in erect position, swing both arms forward and then sideward letting them drop during the swings so that the hands brush the thighs on each motion. An effort should be made to keep the shoulders low. Do not hurry, and continue for half a minute or more.

Kneeling, sitting on a low stool, or standing in erect position, swing both arms from a position with forearms crossed in front of the chest to an attitude with the arms extended in oblique position above and behind the head. Keep the arms moving rhythmically, for several rounds, through the entire arc of motion in the suggested directions.

Sitting on the edge of a chair with one overhanging hand clenched very tightly, swing that arm forcibly in large circles, the right clockwise and the left counterclockwise. Feel as though you are swinging it out of its socket.

Sitting on the edge of a table, with the lower legs hanging free. let the legs swing alternately forward and backward. Keep them moving alternately in rhythm to a simple tune.

This motion will free tautness in the thighs and improve circulation in the legs.

Sitting on the edge of a table, with the lower legs hanging free, swing both legs from side to side in unison. The lower legs will remain parallel.

This motion will free tautness in the region of the hip joints.

Standing with one side close to a table so that the hand on that side may give support, swing the opposite or outside leg forward and backward loosely from the hip joint.

Assuming a position on all fours with knees separated a few inches, with thighs perpendicular to the floor, with the shoulders the same height as the hips and the elbows bent slightly, hump the back and let the head hang down; then extend the spine with the head held high.

Emphasis should be placed on humping or flexing in the lumbar region and lowering or extending in the thoracic region of the spine.

To make this movement a little more difficult, but much more effective for freeing the spinal muscles from the tautness that develops when the trunk is held erect, let the elbows bend and the trunk swing backward when the head is up and the chest is low. Then let the trunk move forward and the arms extend again as the head droops and the back humps.

Kneeling with the feet under the hips and the hands reaching over the head, let the trunk sway and twist so that the hands can transcribe half circles on the floor followed by half circles in the opposite direction in the air. The movements should be full and sweeping, with the trunk moving an equal number of times, in both directions.

Standing with hips supported against the wall, the feet apart and a few inches from the wall, the trunk bent forward and the arms drooping, let the body sway in a semicircle from side to side with arms and head loose.

Standing with the hips supported against the wall, in the same manner as in the previous exercise. Let the trunk make a great circle. The trunk should sway to one side, swing across to the opposite side and be raised with the lateral trunk muscles before drooping down to the starting position. The arms will transcribe an arc in the air from one side to the other, up over the head, and down to the side from which the movement started.

Descent Relaxation (DR)

Settle yourself into a comfortable, seated position, adjust your posture so that the chair is completely supporting your weight. Close your eyes and begin by taking three long slow breaths, focusing on the feeling of relaxation each time as you breathe out. Notice with each breath that you take that there is a moment of relief with the exhalation of each breath.

Continue to breathe slowly, enjoying the feeling of relaxation and as you do, try to associate that pleasant feeling with an increasing heaviness in each muscle group within your body.

Let that feeling begin in the muscles around your forehead and face and then let it spread very slowly down through your neck and shoulders (continue the spread of relaxation taking at least two minutes to spread it down through your whole body).

When you have relaxed each and every muscle group within your body take two more deep breaths and then enjoy the feeling of relaxation.

When you wish to 'reawaken' count slowly backwards from five to one, stretching your muscles as you do so. You will then feel refreshed and rested.

Systematic Loosening (SL)

Left leg: flex the muscles of your left leg by raising it 6–10in above the floor. Point your toes slightly back toward your head. Hold this position of tension for as long as you can, about 10 seconds or so, until you begin to feel the muscles start to tremble. Then say to yourself, 'Leg, let go'.

At this point, stop flexing it and let the leg drop.

Let the leg rest for another 10 seconds or so, saying to yourself, 'I feel the tension flowing out of my leg. My legs feel relaxed, warm, heavy. . . completely relaxed.'

Repeat.

Right leg: run through the entire procedure twice for your right leg.

Buttocks and thighs: tighten your buttock and thigh muscles, as tightly as you can. Hold them as long as you can (longer than 10 seconds) until you have to let go. Then release them saying, 'Let go' to yourself. Pause for 10 seconds or so and focus your attention on the relaxed feeling in those muscles, on the tension flowing out.

Repeat the exercise.

Stomach: do the same procedure twice for your abdominal muscles.

Back and neck: arch your spine, tightening all along it from your tailbone to your neck, and finish by telling it, 'Let go'.

Repeat the exercise.

Arms and shoulders: imagine that there is a bar suspended above you that you want to use it to pull yourself up. Raise your hands, palms upward, above your chest. Grab the imaginary bar and clench your fists around it as hard as you can.

Flex the muscles in your arms and shoulders. Hunch your shoulders up as tightly as you can. Hold as long as possible, then say, 'Let go'.

Rest for 10 seconds or so, soaking up the warm, relaxed feelings, letting the tension flow out.

Repeat the exercise.

Modal Ten Relaxation (MTR)

The basic approach in this technique is to focus on different muscle groups in the order indicated below for between 30 and 90 seconds each. The exercise does not involve any tightening or relaxing of muscle groups. It merely requires that the athlete focus on the amount of relaxation that exists in each of the areas. It is almost as if Modal Ten Relaxation were a somatic check list of how the body is feeling.

The sequence is important and consequently athletes have to learn the routine. This will take some practice. It does not matter if the time spent on each area varies, provided that it falls within the period indicated. The significant thing is not that the muscles are or are not relaxed, but that the athlete can keep his concentration narrowly focused on the physical sensations going to the brain from those muscles.

I ask athletes to imagine that I am going to ask them about the amount of relaxation in each muscle group after the exercise, and that they will have to score themselves on a scale of 1–10 for each area. Initially, at least, I like the athletes to learn Modal Ten Relaxation while lying on a comfortable bed. They begin by being in a symmetrical position with their eyes and mouth closed. The entire process will take between 10 and 12 minutes.

Breathing Control Techniques

Alpha Breathing

Adopt a suitable position: sitting upright, feet flat on the floor, eyes closed.

Take five easy, full breaths and exhale softly each time, saying silently to yourself 'Relax'.

After the fifth breath take another five full breaths to a casual backward count from five to one, continuing to say to yourself 'Relax' with each exhalation.

On the next breath (the eleventh) say 'Five' to yourself as you breathe out; on the twelfth say, 'Four'; and so on down until the fifteenth breath is accompanied by 'One'.

Quiet Breathing

Sit with your eyes and mouth closed, and focus on your breathing rate. To start with, your breaths in and out will sound quite different from each other. Breathing in is usually noisier than breathing out.

This must be corrected and it may need a fair amount of concentration and practice to do so.

When breathing-in quietens, breathing immediately feels better as it loses its characteristic gasping inrush of air.

Model the breathing-in sound on the breathing-out sound.

Pendulum Breathing

Once you have mastered the sound of breathing, the next thing is to concentrate on losing the pauses at full inspiration and at full expiration. Try to imagine the pendulum of a clock. As it reaches the full sweep at one side of its swing it stops momentarily before swinging back.

You cannot actually see it stop, of course, but this momentary pause is exactly the one you are trying to build into your relaxation breathing. This is pendulum breathing.

Centering (see Chapter 2)

Stand with the feet shoulder-width apart.
Relax your shoulders.
Focus on your abdominal 'out' movements as you breathe through the nose.
Notice how your stomach goes out as you breathe in.
Avoid any up and down movement of the shoulders.
Keep your breathing steady and rhythmical.

Modal Ten Breathing

This is performed in the same order as Modal Ten Relaxation.

Stand with the body weight evenly distributed over a firm base and with your mouth closed.

Focus on your breathing, and once you have become 'in tune' with the rate, start on the next inhalation.

The next time you breathe out, say the number 'one' silently to yourself and focus on your stomach muscles. Imagine that someone has painted a large number one on the abdominal muscles.

Then go through the same routine of inhalation/exhalation with superimposed numbers for the parts of the body as if conducting a standard MTR. The entire process will take less than 2 minutes.

Reading List

Bloomfield, J., Fricker, P.A. and Fitch, K.D. (eds.), *Science And Medicine In Sport*, 2nd Edition (Blackwell Science, 1995)

Bull, S.J., Albinson, J.G. and Shambrook, C.J., *The Mental Game Plan* (Sports Dynamics, 1996)

Butler, R. J., *Sports Psychology in Action* (Butterworth-Heinemann, 1996)

Butler, R. J., *Sports Psychology in Performance* (Butterworth-Heinemann, 1997)

Eysenck, M.W., *Anxiety: The Cognitive Perspective* (Lawrence Earlbaum, 1992)

Fazey, J.A. and Hardy, L., BASS Monograph No.1, *The Inverted-U Hypotheses: A Catastrophe for Sports Psychology* (National Coaching Foundation, 1988)

Gordon, S., 'A Mental Skills Training Programme for the Western Australian State Cricket Team', *The Sport Psychologist*, 4, 1990

Gould, D., Eklund, R.C. and Jackson, S.A., '1988 US Olympic wrestling excellence: 1. Mental preparation, precompetitive cognition and affect', *The Sport Psychologist*, 6, 1992

Hardy, L., Jones, G. and Gould, D., *Understanding Psychological Preparation For Sport* (John Wiley & Sons, 1996)

Heil, J., *Psychology of Sport Injury* (Human Kinetic Publishers, 1993)

Hobfoll, S.E. and Stephens, M.A.P., 'Social support during extreme stress: Consequences and intervention', in Sarason, B.R., Sarason, I.G. and Pierce, G.R. (eds.), *Social support: An interactional view* (John Wiley & Sons, 1990)

Horn, T.S. (ed.), *Advances in Sport Psychology* (Human Kinetic Publishers, 1992)

Jackson, S.A. and Roberts, G.C., 'Positive performance states of athletes: towards a conceptual understanding of peak performance', *The Sport Psychologist*, 6, 1992

Jones, G. and Hardy, L. (eds.), *Stress and Performance in Sport* (John Wiley & Sons, 1990)

Kubler-Ross, E. *On Death and Dying* (Macmillan, 1969)

Miller, B.P. 'A Skill Based Approach to Psychological Training in Athletics', *Proceedings of the Second IAAF Medical Congress, Canberra* (1985)

Morris, T. and Summers, J. (eds.).*Sport Psychology: Theory, Application and Issues* (John Wiley & Sons, 1995)

Murphy, S. (ed.), *Sport Psychology Interventions* (Human Kinetics Publishers, 1995)

Nideffer, R.M., 'Test of attentional and interpersonal style', *Journal of Personality and Social Psychology* 34, 1996

Nideffer, R.M., *Psyched to Win* (Leisure Press, 1992)

Orlick, T. and Partington, J., 'Mental links to excellence', *The Sport Psychologist*, 2, 1988

Orlick, T. and Werthner, P., *Athletes in Transition* (Coaching Association of Canada, 1987)

Orlick, T., *In Pursuit of Excellence*, 2nd Edition (Leisure Press, 1991)

Pargman, D. (ed.), *Psychological Bases of Sport Injuries* (Fitness Information Technology, 1993)

Rotella, R.J., 'Psychological care of the injured athlete', in Kulund, D.N. (ed.), *The Injured Athlete* (Lippincott, 1982)

Ryan, J., *Little Girls in Pretty Boxes* (The Women's Press, 1995)

Shaw, M., *Group Dynamics: The Psychology of Small Group Behaviour* (McGraw-Hill, 1976)

Steiner, I., *Group Processes and Productivity* (Academic Press, 1972)

Terry, P., *The Winning Mind* (Thorsons, 1989)

Weiner, B., 'A theory of motivation for some classroom experiences', *Journal of Educational Psychology*, 71, 1979

Williams, J.M. (ed.), *Applied Sport Psychology* (Mayfield, 1986)

Index